THE SCHOOL AND SOCIETY

and

THE CHILD AND THE CURRICULUM

The
SCHOOL
and
SOCIETY

BEING THREE LECTURES

by

JOHN DEWEY

PROFESSOR OF PEDAGOGY IN
THE UNIVERSITY OF CHICAGO

SUPPLEMENTED BY
A STATEMENT OF
THE UNIVERSITY
ELEMENTARY SCHOOL

1 9 0 0
CHICAGO
THE UNIVERSITY OF CHICAGO PRESS
NEW YORK
McCLURE, PHILLIPS & COMPANY

THE SCHOOL AND SOCIETY

and

THE CHILD AND THE CURRICULUM

JOHN DEWEY

INTRODUCTION BY PHILIP W. JACKSON

A Centennial Publication
of the University of Chicago Press

THE UNIVERSITY OF CHICAGO PRESS

CHICAGO & LONDON

THE UNIVERSITY OF CHICAGO PRESS, CHICAGO 60637
The University of Chicago Press, Ltd., London

The Child and the Curriculum: Copyright 1902 by The University of Chicago.
The School and Society: Copyright 1900, 1915 (revised edition), 1943 by John
Dewey.

LIBRARY OF CONGRESS CATALOGING-IN-PUBLICATION DATA
Dewey, John, 1859–1952.
    [School and society]
    The school and society; and, The child and the curriculum : a
centennial edition with a "lost essay" / by John Dewey and a new
introduction by Philip W. Jackson.
        p. cm.
    Reprint. Originally published: 1956.
    ISBN 0-226-14395-3 (cloth). — ISBN 0-226-14396-1 (pbk.)
    1. Education—Philosophy. 2. Educational sociology. 3. Child
development. 4. Education—Aims and objectives. 5. University of
Chicago. Laboratory Schools—History. I. Dewey, John, 1859–1952.
Child and the curriculum. 1990. II. Title. III. Title: School and
society. IV. Title: Child and the curriculum.
LB875.D4 1990
370'.1—dc20   90-43528
                                                                      CIP

♾ The paper used in this publication meets the minimum requirements of the
American National Standard for Information Sciences—Permanence of Paper
for Printed Library Materials, ANSI Z39.48–1984.

Contents

The School and Society
List of Illustrations

Introduction

This volume contains two of the most widely read and highly acclaimed educational treatises of the twentieth century. To all who care about the history of educational thought that fact alone should be reason enough for wanting to read or re-read both *The School and Society* and *The Child and the Curriculum*. Readers oriented toward practice will likely have a different incentive for turning to these two well-known essays. They will want to mine them for ideas that might be applied in today's schools. They too should not be disappointed by what they find in the pages to follow.

There is an additional reason, however, for reexamining both texts at this distance in time, one that may entice some readers (as it did me) fully as much as do their historical significance and the likelihood of their containing ideas that will be of immediate use. This is the possibility that one or both of these brief monographs may be found to contain the answer or at least part of the answer to a question that has long puzzled Dewey's admirers. The question is this: Why hasn't Dewey's influence as an educator been as widespread and enduring as he and others had initially hoped it would be? Why haven't more of his ideas been put into practice? As one friendly commentator, Arthur G. Wirth, remarked in 1966, "More than six decades [beyond its inception], Dewey's ideal is more relevant than ever, yet still remains to be realized. A full accounting for the limited progress to date constitutes one of the sorely needed studies about twentieth-century American education" (1966, 71). An identical judgment would not be out of place today as we approach the one-hundredth anniversary of these seminal works.

To suggest that part of the answer to the question of Dewey's limited influence may reside within the texts contained in this volume is not to deny the near certainty of there being other sources of the difficulty as well, some of which may be far more explanatory than anything to be found in the texts themselves. Wirth, for one, immediately following the passage that has just been quoted, went on to suggest that "the pressures of an expanding educational system" may have been too great to accommodate Dewey's notions (71). He also expressed the hope that "an imaginative use of new technology may bring the ideal closer to our grasp" (71). Others have concluded that the practices Dewey advocated were far too demanding for the average teacher (Schwab 1978). There may even be some, though I cannot readily name any of their number, who believe that the only thing preventing the ultimate realization of Dewey's vision is the absence of the will and determination to get the job done. Each of today's readers of *The School and Society* and *The Child and the Curriculum* will doubtless come to his or her own conclusions about the attractiveness and feasibility of the educational ideas those writings contain. If my own experience is any guide, a reading of both monographs guided by the question of whether Dewey's views might suffer from some kind of internal weaknesses should prove to be rewarding. What that perspective made clear for me, among other things, was how central Dewey's notion of a laboratory school was to the fulfillment of his broader educational goals. I came to see how the fate of Dewey's educational ideas were inextricably tied to the fate of his own experimental school, not simply in the way hypotheses are tied to the outcomes of investigations but in subtler and more complex ways as well. The key determinant of the success of Dewey's venture into educational practice, I now believe, has to do with the conception of what a laboratory school might accomplish. To explain how I arrived at that conviction, which I offer not as the gospel truth but as a provocative outlook whose controversial nature should encourage others to develop views of their own, I must present a few elementary facts about the school Dewey founded, most of which are doubtless familiar to some readers but probably not to all.

John Dewey, who joined the faculty of the University of Chicago in 1894 as professor of philosophy, psychology, and pedagogy, founded the University Elementary School, as it was first called, in 1896. It was officially renamed the Laboratory School in 1902, a name retained to this day, though the singular noun "School" has since been replaced by the plural "Schools" as a consequence of the institution's expanding to include four components—nursery, elementary, middle, and high—whose union forms a single educational complex.

The University of Chicago Laboratory Schools of today are widely considered, individually and collectively, to be among the very best independent schools in the city. They currently enroll more than fourteen hundred students, virtually all of whom will go on to college, many to prestigious schools. By all of the statistical criteria commonly used to judge educational quality—SAT scores, number of Merit Scholars, number of applicants seeking admission, and so forth—today's Laboratory Schools receive high marks. Thus, from a materialistic, quantitative point of view it would appear as though Dewey's modest experiment, which began with only fifteen students, housed in rented space, has unquestionably flourished in the years since its founding.

Appearances can be deceiving, however, as we all know. For if we restrict ourselves to a comparison between the kind of school Dewey was trying to develop, the one whose early years of operation are described in this volume, and the Laboratory Schools as they exist today, we come up with a very different judgment about the long-term success of Dewey's experiment. Whatever else today's Laboratory Schools might be, they certainly are not the educational laboratory their founder envisioned. What has disappeared over the years is not the institution itself, which, if anything, seems to have prospered. What is missing today is the schools' entitlement to the key word "laboratory" that continues to define the kind of school it purports to be.

Moreover, it is not just the laboratory-ness of the University of Chicago Laboratory Schools that has disappeared. The category of which it was the founding member has suffered a drastic reduction in membership. That too has been a disappearance of sorts. As the notoriety of the Chicago experiment slowly spread, a number of schools around the country, following Dewey's lead, began to call themselves laboratory schools and openly aspired to the same goals that Dewey and his staff had espoused. Those schools have today all but vanished and, of the handful that remain, it is doubtful that any one of them continues to deserve being called a laboratory in the Deweyan sense, if indeed it ever did. In brief, what has all but gone today is the institutional enactment of Dewey's initial idea of a laboratory school as a place with a very special kind of educational mission. Why might that have happened? What, if anything, was wrong with the idea?

To pursue those questions in our reading of *The School and Society* and *The Child and the Curriculum* we need to begin our investigation by taking a close look at the early days of the Dewey School, shortly before the word "laboratory" appeared in its title. What we quickly discover when we do so (possibly to no one's surprise) is that from the very beginning financial considerations loomed large in the minds of those university officials who had to approve the school's budget. Such considerations cast a threatening shadow over the institution's future almost before it got underway. Indeed, as early as three years after its founding, which means even before Dewey delivered the talks to "parents and friends of the school" that were to comprise *The School and Society,* Dewey's educational experiment was already in financial hot water and had been for some time.

The monetary facts are briefly these: starting with a yearly expenditure of "between $1,300 and $1,400," the school's operating costs had risen steadily as enrollment increased. The cost per student, however, at least according to Dewey, remained relatively constant from year to year (1900, 114). By the end of the third year annual expenses were estimated to be "about $12,000," of which $5,500 was to come from tuition and $5,000 from "friends interested in the school," leaving $1,500 "yet to be raised" (1900, 114). In light of this condition, William Rainey Harper, then president of the University of Chicago, proposed that Dewey substantially increase both tuition (which then covered only about half the actual cost per pupil) and class size (the pupil/teacher ratio was then about 9 or 10 to 1). Dewey agreed to the former strategy but resisted the latter, a compromise that promised to reduce the financial problem but not to eliminate it. For even with increased tuition the school would still run a deficit each year that would have to be made up somehow. In the spring of 1899, just about the time of Dewey's *The School and Society* talks, an impending deficit of $1,200 for the school year then ending, which amounted to about one-tenth of the school's annual costs, led President Harper to make a special appeal to potential donors to help balance the books before the trustees were asked to approve the coming year's budget. As an expression of his personal support of the project, Harper contributed $100 of his own (McCaul 1961).

The key question to which these financial disclosures give rise is why a university should choose to fund such an enterprise in the first place. The historical evidence suggests that President Harper and the university trustees never intended to provide more than what today would be called "seed money" to get the project underway. They were quite willing to have the school associated with the university and, as Harper's personal donation reveals, some were even prepared to contribute money of their own to its upkeep. But they clearly did not wish the newly founded school to become a continuing drain (even if a modest one) on the university's resources. Dewey, on the other hand, thought that the university should willingly bear a portion of the school's costs. He argued that "money should be spent (as) freely for the organization and maintenance of foundation work in education [by which he meant the earliest years of schooling] as . . . for the later stages" (1900, 115). But at the same time he clearly recognized that "[t]he aim of educating a certain number of children would hardly justify a university in departing from the tradition which limits it to those who have completed their secondary instruction" (96; all undated Dewey references are to the current edition).

Why, then, should his own institution, the University of Chicago, veer from that tradition? There is but one answer to that question, Dewey insisted. "Only the scientific aim, the conduct of a laboratory, comparable to other scientific laboratories, can furnish a reason for the maintenance by a university of an elementary school" (96). Thus, he concluded, "[f]rom the university standpoint the most important part of [the school's] work is the scientific—the contribution it makes to the progress of educational thinking" (96). The import of that answer for the future of Dewey's own school and for schools of like character elsewhere can hardly be exaggerated.

Leaving aside the university administration's worries about money, here was a reply designed to squelch whatever misgivings President Harper and his trustees might have had over the prospect of having an elementary school in their midst. Its rhetorical appeal was made to order. After all, the university presumably did not hesitate to provide laboratories for each of the major sciences. Indeed, the fledgling institution, cast in the model of German research universities, prided itself on the presence of such facilities. Why not, then, a school that was also a laboratory, one in which, as Dewey explained, "the student of education sees theories and ideas demonstrated, tested, criticized, enforced, and the evolution of new truths" (93)?

Few supporters of the university's founding ideals could possibly oppose such a proposal. Moreover, lest anyone think that Dewey was merely indulging in metaphor when he spoke of creating a "laboratory school," key passages within his appeal, such as the one just quoted, made it clear that he was not. He meant the word "laboratory" to be taken literally. But therein lies the tantalizing question: how literal can the analogy between the two kinds of institutions actually be? Under what conditions, if any, can a school become a laboratory?

Before we seek to address that question directly it is worth noting that history proved Dewey wrong in his insistence that a "scientific aim" provides the *only* reason for a university to tolerate an elementary school in its midst. Dewey himself may have been unable to think of any other legitimating reason for such an arrangement but his own university's officials had no trouble doing so, as local events were soon to reveal. Only two or three years after Dewey's "scientific aim" remark a *second* elementary school arrived on campus, soon to be followed by not one but two secondary schools. The new elementary unit was a part of Colonel Francis Parker's training school for teachers, which had been brought to campus at the insistence of Mrs. Emmons Blaine, whose offer of funds for a building to house the enterprise was accepted by President Harper. Parker's elementary school was explicitly designed to be a *demonstration* school, which was definitely not the kind of institution that Dewey had in mind. The two high schools, one focused on manual training, the other more of an academy for the college-bound, were also unlike the kind of educational laboratory that Dewey conceived of creating. Furthermore, the fact that the University of Chicago Laboratory Schools enjoy continuing financial support from the university to this day yet can no longer be considered to be either demonstration schools *or* laboratory schools in the Deweyan sense only confirms what was evident even in Dewey's day, which is that there exists not one or even two but probably a host of reasons why a university might choose to maintain an elementary or high school in its environs. Insofar as today's Laboratory Schools are concerned, the chief reason for continuing university support appears to be that the schools have proved to be useful over the years in attracting new faculty members to the university and in keeping a significant portion of the faculty and other middle-class families residing in the neighborhood, thereby enriching the local community and contributing to its stability.

Returning to the laboratory analogy, we are now in a position to ask: How closely and in what ways was Dewey's school to resemble a scientific laboratory? Dewey's own remarks about how the school was to operate provide part of the answer. "Its task," he said, "is the problem of viewing the education of the child in the light of the principles of mental activity and the processes of growth made known by modern psychology" (96–97). This would make the school, in Dewey's terms, "a laboratory of applied psychology" (96).

Elsewhere Dewey spoke of his school as incorporating a number of "sociological principles" as well as psychological ones (Wirth 1966, 297). The former called for developing within the school "a *community* of spirit and end" intermediate between the family and other, larger social organizations (298). The school was also to be "a working model of a unified education," an elementary school nested within the confines of a university that itself aspired to become one of the great research institutions of the world (Dewey, 93). Such an arrangement, Dewey felt, would "break down the barriers that divide the education of the little child from the instruction of the maturing youth, [thus demonstrating] to the eye that there is no lower or higher, but simply education" (92). Moreover, even in this limited sense of "model" the school was not designed for others to emulate, for as Dewey went on to say, "We do not expect to have other schools literally imitate what we do. A working model is not something to be copied; it is to afford a demonstration of the feasibility of the principle and of the methods which make it feasible" (94).

What emerges from this string of quotations is a sense of there being not one but two interrelated yet distinguishably different sets of activities that, for Dewey, justified calling his school a laboratory. One dealt with the experimental application of psychological principles to educational practice. The other sought to instantiate a number of sociological insights that stressed the essential continuity of educational concepts and practices across the spectrum of human development, from the school experiences of the very young child to those of the mature student.

The psychological principles that Dewey hoped to see applied in the classrooms of his school were quite unlike those current in the field of psychology today. This is not at all surprising of course, given the passage of time. Moreover, the embryonic status of this budding young science at the time of Dewey's educational experiment is also noteworthy. If we date the emergence of modern psychology with the establishment of Wilhelm Wundt's laboratory in Leipzig in 1875, as historians of science customarily do, psychology would have been only slightly more than twenty years old when Dewey founded his school.

Dewey's psychology, at least that portion of it that he saw as having educational relevance, was more a point of view than an integrated assemblage of empirically grounded facts and principles. It was an outlook on human nature, one that depicted humans as actively striving to explore and to master their world rather than passively reacting to forces impinging upon them from the outside. It viewed them as being driven by natural instincts and interests, rather than as seeking peace and quiescence. Dewey spoke of this point of view as constituting "a radically different psychology" (104), one that would ultimately replace "the psychology of former days" (98). The latter view, according to Dewey, looked upon "mind as a purely individual affair in direct and naked contact with an external world" (98). It was "a psychology of knowledge, of intellect," one in which "[e]motion and endeavor occupied but an incidental and derivative place" (101). Finally, the old view had no room for a conception of mind as a process of growth. Instead, as Dewey puts it, "mind was mind, and that was the whole story" (102).

There are two things to say about Dewey's "new" psychology that may help to contextualize it. The first is that as a broad perspective on the human condition, leaving aside its status as "science," it was really not all that new. The dual notion, 1) that humans, and especially young children, are active and curious by nature and 2) that educators need to take cognizance of that fact, figured prominently in the writings of Rousseau, Pestalozzi, Froebel, and numerous other educational thinkers long before the emergence of modern psychology. Moreover, it is not entirely clear what the findings of the embryonic new science of psychology had by Dewey's day added to that historically venerated perspective, if indeed they had added anything at all. Only a few years prior to Dewey's educational venture no less prominent a spokesman for modern psychology than William James had openly declared that, "in my humble opinion there *is* no 'new psychology' worthy of the name" (1901, 7). James went on to say,

> There is nothing but the old psychology which began in
> Locke's time, plus a little physiology of the brain and senses
> and theory of evolution, and a few refinements of introspec-
> tive detail, for the most part without adaptation to the teach-
> er's use. It is only the fundamental conceptions of psychology
> which are of real value to the teacher; and they, apart from the
> aforesaid theory of evolution, are very far from being new. (7)

The point of introducing James's observation is not to place stress on the fact that he and Dewey were in disagreement, though they obviously were in some respects. Rather it is to emphasize what has already been said, which is that around the turn of the century there were not very many new psychological findings and principles to apply to educational affairs. Dewey acknowledged that that was so. He admitted that few of the "psychological facts," which would comprise the building blocks of this "new psychology," were yet in place. He then went on to point out, however, that educators had a lot of work to do on their own, calling it "clear presumption" to claim that they yet knew how to develop materials and methods of instruction that were "in harmony" with what was already known. At the same time, he insisted that what *was* known was sufficient to make "intelligent inquiry" possible. He further believed that such inquiry offered "the only step which can introduce rational conviction into education" (104). Such was Dewey's conception of the work to be accomplished by a laboratory school.

The second point to be made about Dewey's perspective on psychology is that it was not the *only* view that could be taken, as was made evident by the fact that it was offered as a replacement for an older, presumably outmoded psychology. More importantly, however, it was not the point of view that was to grow in dominance as the new science matured. Shortly after the turn of the century British associationism was to provide the groundwork for the emergence of a stimulus-response psychology that would later develop into a form of behaviorism which would become the dominant outlook among psychologists for at least fifty years. This is not to say that the view Dewey championed was to disappear completely. On the contrary, its advocates, who later were to march under an assortment of banners, including "gestalt," "dynamic," and "humanistic" psychology, remained numerous during the heyday of behaviorism, even though they were greatly outnumbered. What we need to keep in mind, however, is that almost from the start Dewey's outlook was a *contested* point of view.

There is an additional observation to make about the task that Dewey set for himself and his teachers. It grows out of the fact that the "psychological principles" on which he sought to base the work of his school were not only few in number (They "might almost be written on the palm of one's hand," William James had insisted [12]) but also quite general in character. The difficulty with using so few and such general principles as a foundation for practice is that they are insufficiently numerous and detailed to give much guidance (or constraint) to the practitioner. Again we turn to James for insight into the problem.

"A science only lays down lines within which the rules of the art must fall," James observed, "laws which the follower of the art must not transgress; but what particular thing he shall positively do within those lines is left exclusively to his own genius" (8). James then went on to say what this meant for the relationship between psychology and teaching. "And so everywhere the teaching must *agree* with the psychology," he explained, "but need not necessarily be the only kind of teaching that would so agree; for many diverse methods of teaching may equally well agree with psychological laws" (8–9). James thought that psychology might actually be of greater use in telling teachers what *not* to do than in giving them positive guidance. "We know in advance, if we are psychologists," he said, "that certain methods will be wrong, so our psychology saves us from mistakes" (11).

In fairness to Dewey it must be said that he did not envision a one-to-one correspondence between psychological principles on the one hand and educational practices on the other. Nor did he anticipate providing practitioners with precise directions about how to teach or how to run a school. "A working model is not something to be copied," as we have already heard him explain, "it is to afford a demonstration of the feasibility of the principle and of the methods which make it feasible" (94). How this might work is easy to envision in the abstract. If, for example, we begin with a view of humans that depicts them as being inherently active and engaged, the educational challenge then becomes one of seeing how that view can be put into practice without at the same time sacrificing those outcomes of education that society as a whole wishes to see accomplished. Once the harmonious establishment of the new view and the old goals has been achieved within a single school, assuming that to be possible, it remains for others to develop their own set of practices to accomplish the same results. They may or may not wish to copy the "solution" worked out in the initial, experimental setting but at least they now know that it *can* be done and, thus, are no longer free to dismiss the idea as being scatterbrained or "academic" or just plain unworkable. However, as sensible as this plan may sound when stated succinctly and abstractly, it does not really escape being handicapped by the paucity of psychological principles that Dewey had to work with nor does it overcome the handicap of working with principles that are so general in nature that, as William James had pointed out, they might support "many diverse methods of teaching."

There are two issues involved here, both of which bear on the relationship between a school and a laboratory. One derives from the paucity of psychological principles. If there truly are very few such principles to be applied to education, as James clearly insists there are and as Dewey himself suggests, why is it necessary to establish something as solid and long-lasting as a laboratory in which to work them out? In short, is there enough work to be done to justify such an enduring venture? The other issue concerns the range of inventiveness that remains once Dewey and his teachers have completed their "experiment." Again, if there truly are many different ways of putting the same psychological principles into action, as both Dewey and James aver, what is the advantage of demonstrating within a single school a very limited set of options?

One obvious answer to that last question is that it takes but a single working out of such a plan to establish what Dewey liked to call "the feasibility of the principle." But that rejoinder, which would be fine in situations where feasibility alone was at issue, runs into difficulty when applied to educational affairs. It does so because the important question for practicing educators is seldom if ever "Can this or that innovative practice be shown to work under any circumstances whatsoever?" Of much more interest is whether or not the practice can be put to work back home, in a situation that may be quite unlike the one in which it was initially demonstrated. The key issue, in other words, is rarely feasibility per se. Instead, what is crucial is the range of conditions under which the recommended innovation might reasonably be expected to operate.

This crucial consideration takes us to the heart of the difference between a school that calls itself a laboratory and one that does not. It brings to our attention an additional difficulty with which Dewey and all future heads of laboratory schools had to cope, one that Dewey himself appears not to have foreseen as clearly as he might have done. A major difficulty that faces laboratory schools everywhere is one of convincing visitors and others who have only heard about the school's operations that what goes on there can be emulated elsewhere. What makes this difficult is the fact that laboratories of whatever kind are, by definition, very special places and are so in a variety of ways.

To begin with, they are *refined* or *purified* environments, places where the racket and din of the workaday world have been at least partially reduced, where not only noise and dirt but also their ideational equivalents—confusion and disorder—can be filtered out or systematically controlled. They are also *reflective* environments, places where people have time to think carefully about what they are doing, time to reflect upon the outcomes of their actions and to plan next steps with caution and care. They are *semipublic* environments in that those who work within them are under obligation of either a moral or contractual kind to report on their findings and to open their facility to inspection if called upon to do so. They are, additionally, *risk-taking* environments, places where new and sometimes risky ventures are undertaken and where the possibility of failure is openly acknowledged. Finally, most laboratories are also *expensive* environments, made so by the costs of maintaining the conditions just named. Those costs commonly include not only the purchase of expensive equipment and the facility in which it is to be housed but also the salaries of highly skilled personnel and the support services they require.

Such demands naturally vary. Not all laboratories are equally rigorous in their adherence to these various standards. Some require more antiseptic conditions than do others. The activities within some are fast-paced in tempo; within others they are slow. Some are open to the public; others operate in secrecy. Some are crowded with equipment and technicians; others are not. Some court the risk of failure and even of physical danger much of the time; others are as benign and as safe as a scholar's study.

Those laboratories that are avowedly devoted to applied studies of various kinds, as Dewey wanted his school to be, often go to great lengths to simulate conditions of the outside world. The experimental kitchens of food manufacturers and the out-of-doors proving grounds for the road-testing of motor vehicles spring immediately to mind as examples of this type. But the "natural" conditions so necessary for the testing of products in these applied laboratories does not bring them closer to the ordinary in any of the other dimensions along which dissimilarities with ordinary environments are common.

What of Dewey's laboratory school? How different was it from schools in general? It is hard to answer that question solely on the basis of what is reported in *The School and Society* and *The Child and the Curriculum*. But by using the information those texts provide, plus a little extra from such readily accessible accounts of the school as that of Mayhew and Edwards (1936), one can at least make a few educated guesses about some of the major differences. It is known, for example, that the pupil/teacher ratio during the first few years of the school's operation was about nine or ten to one. We also know that the school was situated in a community that placed a very high premium on the value of education and one in which an experimental attitude was not only tolerated but highly prized. Judging from the volume of reports that issued from the school during those early years, some written by Dewey and others by his staff, it is evident that an appreciable amount of time was spent in staff discussions and planning sessions and in reflecting both individually and collectively on what was going on. This activity speaks, of course, not only to the dedication of the staff but also to the intellectual caliber of many if not most of the participants. We know that when the school was finally permanently housed it had ample outdoor space for gardens and playing fields and was generously equipped with laboratories and shops. We are not told very much about the student body of the school but judging from the snippets of essays and student artwork contained in *The School and Society*, plus the fact that tuition was charged, we may safely guess that the school served what today would be called a middle-class clientele, which would include, we might readily surmise, a number of children whose mother or father (far more likely the latter) was on the faculty of the university. We know, for example, that Dewey's own children attended the school.

What all of this adds up to is the recognition that Dewey's school was a very special place indeed and was so in many of the same ways that laboratories in general are special. It was, in short, a privileged environment. Dewey readily acknowledged this state of affairs and was quick to defend the school's special status. Consider, for example, his response to what sounds as though it might have been a standard complaint of at least some visitors to his school. "I heard once," he said, "that the adoption of a certain method in use in our school was objected to by a teacher on this ground: 'You know that it is an experimental school. They do not work under the same conditions that we are subject to'" (93). How does Dewey deal with that complaint? Unfortunately, he does not do so at all, at least not directly. Indeed, there is a sense in which he seems not to have heard the teacher's objection, for he goes on without pause to say, "Now the purpose of performing an experiment is that other people need not experiment; at least need not experiment so much, may have something definite and positive to go by. An experiment demands particularly favorable conditions in order that results may be reached both freely and securely. It has to work unhampered, with all the needed resources at command" (93–94). The question he fails to address, however, which is the one that seems to have prompted the teacher's observation, is whether some of those "particularly favorable conditions" and "needed resources" might also be required to put the same principles into practice somewhere else. To allay the visitor's concern on that score he would either have had to show that the difference between his school and hers was really not that great after all, which surely would have been difficult to do for reasons that have already been stated, or he would have had to argue that whatever differences there might be were irrelevant because they did not affect the practical application of the principle in question, which seems an equally improbable argument to make.

When we think of the many advantages enjoyed by both teachers and students in Dewey's school we can easily begin to sympathize with the visitor's complaint. An unusually small teacher/pupil ratio, a dedicated and enthusiastic staff with time to reflect on what they were doing, well-behaved and eager students, an encouraging administrator, a supportive institutional environment, the backing of enthused parents, adequate materials and ample physical space— these well may be "needed resources" for the operation of an educational laboratory, as Dewey likely would have insisted, but they are also among the ingredients that contribute to educational excellence no matter where it is found. Such advantages may not in themselves guarantee a fine education but they certainly help to make it probable.

To better understand the visitor's reservations, consider also what the example of Dewey's school was implicitly asking her to do. It was calling upon her to abandon pedagogical practices that were considered by many to be tried and true—activities such as drill, recitation, rote memorization, lecturing, total class instruction, blackboard exercises, and much else that had become routinized and habitual in most schools. It was suggesting that in their place she introduce broad-scale and open-ended group projects that involved activities such as carpentry, weaving, cooking, and candlemaking. It was also recommending that time be spent outside the classroom in planting, building, nature walks, and neighborhood excursions. Moreover, what was being changed were not just the activities, important as they were, but additionally the goals that those activities were designed to serve. It wasn't so much that Dewey was asking for the traditional outcomes of schooling to be abandoned. He supported the necessity of acquiring quite a lot of factual knowledge, for example. But what he did insist upon was that many of these traditional goals could better be achieved if treated secondarily, which meant being subsumed under a broadened vision of what education was all about. Small wonder that some of the school's visitors dragged their heels a bit when it came to trying out back home the practices they had witnessed. Nor is it surprising that they gave as their excuse for doing so their own lack of the clear advantages that Dewey and his staff enjoyed.

In sum, Dewey wanted to make modern psychology the foundation of educational practice but his psychological building blocks were few in number and empirically unsound to boot. Moreover, his were not the only practices that could be derived from such foundations. Further, he championed the necessity of educational experimentation and sought to create in his own school the conditions that would foster it, but those very conditions made his school so special that it became relatively easy and ultimately commonplace to dismiss what went on there as impractical or as not transferable to other, more ordinary, settings.

These were some of the hindrances that stood in the way of Dewey's realizing his dream of a laboratory school. These difficulties, I believe, also help to explain why his educational views have been praised more than practiced, both then and now.

Given this account of all that stood in Dewey's way, we well might ask why the school created such a stir during its early years and why, even now, almost a century later, reports of what went on back then continue to stir the imagination of educationally inquisitive readers. The answers to those questions are varied. They range from the cynical to the idealistic. On the cynical side are explanations of a kind that are put forward to account for why people who live in cramped apartments read *House and Garden* or why throngs flock to auto shows or visit contractors' dream houses or go window-shopping even when they lack the funds to purchase most of the things they see. People simply enjoy looking upon the goods of life, even when or perhaps especially when they can't have those goods themselves. So it must have been with the many idly curious who came to visit Dewey's school during the years when Dewey himself was at its helm and so it probably still is with many who come to visit today's Laboratory Schools, which continue to attract their share of onlookers.

Now as then, the schools remain a kind of tourist attraction. That fact alone suffices to bring in a certain number of visitors.

There is another reason, however, for going out of one's way to visit the school when Dewey was in charge and for wanting to read today about how it was back then. What drew serious students of education to the project from the very beginning and what continues to attract today's readers of these two texts is the pull of an educational vision, a dream, one might say, of what schools everywhere might become through concentrated effort. But the dream extends beyond schooling. It is also a vision of what our whole society might be like if we all worked at it and of how our schools might contribute to that noble end.

Such a vision animated Dewey long before he undertook his educational experiment. Moreover, it did so even more compellingly, I suspect, than did the prospect of establishing an educational laboratory, though the latter possibility certainly had its attractions. To call Dewey's vision a dream, as I have just done, is actually unfair, for it was not at all dreamlike in its day-to-day functioning. Dewey would have called it an end-in-view and so it was at the time: an ideal that served as a guide to action, one whose realization occurred by degrees and whose perceivable form and shape were themselves being constantly modified by the actual course of events.

The school Dewey dreamed of (again that inappropriate word intrudes) was one in which old divisions and separations had been overcome or had otherwise disappeared. Gone were to be the barriers and artificial hindrances that long had separated school and society, the child and the curriculum. Gone too were to be the airtight compartments of work and play, thought and action, cognition and volition, and of all the other dichotomies we so commonly use to categorize and ultimately to isolate the polarities of human experience. His was to be a school whose inhabitants—students and teachers alike—were invited to find both personal fulfillment and social well-being in their daily activity, a place where the ultimate test of knowledge was to be its usefulness but where the useful was to include the aesthetic, the contemplative, and what some would call the spiritual aspects of human experience.

What shall we make of Dewey's ideal today? Was it too utopian? Can a version of it still be achieved? Was his vision handicapped by being tied to the idea of a laboratory? Might he have done better to forgo his talk of the "scientific aim" of such a school and to concentrate instead on the avowedly idealistic portrayal of the educationally attainable? These are questions whose answers are still open. They are also ones that remain of vital significance to both educators and our citizenry at large. Though the approaching centennial of Dewey's many contributions to education makes today's contemplation of these matters timely, the questions themselves deal with issues that surely will be pondered for decades to come. Read on and decide for yourself what their answers might be.

Philip W. Jackson

References

Dewey, John. 1900. *The School and Society.* Chicago: University of Chicago Press.

Dewey, John. 1902. *The Child and the Curriculum.* Chicago: University of Chicago Press.

Dewey, John. [1900,1902] 1956. *The Child and the Curriculum and The School and Society.* Combined Edition. Chicago: University of Chicago Press.

James, William. 1901. *Talks to Teachers on Psychology: and to Students on Some of Life's Ideals.* New York: Henry Holt.

Mayhew, Katherine Camp, and Anna Camp Edwards. 1936. *The Dewey School.* New York, London: D. Appleton-Century.

McCaul, Robert L. 1961. Dewey and the University of Chicago. *School and Society* 89:152–57, 179–83, 202–6.

Schwab, Joseph J. 1978. *Science, Curriculum, and Liberal Education.* Ed. Ian Westbury and Neil J. Wilkof. Chicago: University of Chicago Press.

Wirth, Arthur G. 1966. *John Dewey as Educator.* New York: John Wiley and Sons.

Note on the Publishing History of the Text and on This Edition

In April of 1899 John Dewey gave three lectures before an audience of "parents and others interested in the University of Chicago Elementary School," the school that he had founded three years prior. In November of that same year those lectures, together with a stenographic report of a talk entitled "Three Years of the University Elementary School," also by Dewey, appeared as *The School and*

Society, a publication of the University of Chicago Press. The sales of that slim volume were remarkable from the start. The first printing of one thousand copies was followed three months later by a second run of fifteen hundred. Four months after that, in July of 1900, an additional five thousand copies were run off, making a total of seventy-five hundred copies in print before the book was a year old.

Over the years that followed, *The School and Society* went through dozens of further printings before it was revised by Dewey in 1915. The revised version, which contained five additional chapters of Dewey's writings that had first appeared in the *Elementary Record* and which omitted the report initially included on the first three years of the Elementary School, remained widely read for decades. In 1956 the University of Chicago Press reissued in a single volume *The School and Society* and *The Child and the Curriculum,* another of Dewey's early educational treatises, which had been written about two years after the first set of lectures. As they appeared in that volume the historical order of the two monographs was reversed, with *The Child and the Curriculum* preceding *The School and Society.*

In the present edition the historical order of original appearance of the two monographs has been restored as has the essay entitled "Three Years of the University Elementary School," which had been omitted from printings of *The School and Society* since the revised version of 1915.

P.W.J.

THE SCHOOL AND SOCIETY

Author's Note

A second printing affords a grateful opportunity for recalling that this little book is a sign of the co-operating thoughts and sympathies of many persons. Its indebtedness to Mrs. Emmons Blaine is partly indicated in the dedication. From my friends Mr. and Mrs. George Herbert Mead came that interest, unflagging attention to detail, and artistic taste which, in my absence, re-made colloquial remarks until they were fit to print, and then saw the results through the press with the present attractive result—a mode of authorship made easy, which I recommend to others fortunate enough to possess such friends.

It would be an extended paragraph which should list all the friends whose timely and persisting generosity has made possible the school* which inspired and defined the ideas of these pages. These friends, I am sure, would be the first to recognize the peculiar appropriateness of especial mention of the names of Mrs. Charles R. Crane and Mrs. William R. Linn.

And the school itself in its educational work is a joint undertaking. Many have engaged in shaping it. The clear and experienced intelligence of my wife is wrought everywhere into its texture. The wisdom, tact, and devotion of its instructors have brought about a transformation of its original amorphous plans into articulate form and substance with life and movement of their own. Whatever the issue of the ideas presented in this book, the satisfaction coming from the co-operation of the diverse thoughts and deeds of many persons in undertaking to enlarge the life of the child will abide.

* [PUBLISHER'S NOTE.—The first three chapters appearing here were first delivered as lectures before an audience of parents and others interested in the University of Chicago Elementary School, in April, 1899.]

Author's Note to Second Edition

The present edition includes some slight verbal revisions of the three lectures constituting the first portion of the book. The latter portion is included for the first time, containing material borrowed, with some changes, from the author's contributions to the *Elementary School Record*, long out of print.

The writer may perhaps be permitted a word to express his satisfaction that the educational point of view presented in this book is not so novel as it was fifteen years ago; and his desire to believe that the educational experiment of which the book is an outgrowth has not been without influence in the change.

J. D.

NEW YORK CITY
July, 1915

I
The School and Social Progress

We are apt to look at the school from an individualistic stand-point, as something between teacher and pupil, or between teacher and parent. That which interests us most is naturally the progress made by the individual child of our acquaintance, his normal physical development, his advance in ability to read, write, and figure, his growth in the knowledge of geography and history, improvement in manners, habits of promptness, order, and industry—it is from such standards as these that we judge the work of the school. And rightly so. Yet the range of the outlook needs to be enlarged. What the best and wisest parent wants for his own child, that must the community want for all of its children. Any other ideal for our schools is narrow and unlovely; acted upon, it destroys our democracy. All that society has accomplished for itself is put, through the agency of the school, at the disposal of its future members. All its better thoughts of itself it hopes to realize through the new possibilities thus opened to its future self. Here individualism and socialism are at one. Only by being true to the full growth of all the individuals who make it up, can society by any chance be true to itself. And in the self-direction thus given, nothing counts as much as the school, for, as Horace Mann said, "Where anything is growing, one former is worth a thousand re-formers."

Whenever we have in mind the discussion of a new movement in education, it is especially necessary to take the broader, or social, view. Otherwise, changes in the school institution and tradition will be looked at as the arbitrary inventions of particular teachers, at the worst transitory fads, and at the best merely improvements in certain details—and this is the plane upon which it is too customary to consider school changes. It is as rational to conceive of the locomotive or the telegraph as personal devices.

The modification going on in the method and curriculum of education is as much a product of the changed social situation, and as much an effort to meet the needs of the new society that is forming, as are changes in modes of industry and commerce.

It is to this, then, that I especially ask your attention: the effort to conceive what roughly may be termed the "New Education" in the light of larger changes in society. Can we connect this "New Education" with the general march of events? If we can, it will lose its isolated character; it will cease to be an affair which proceeds only from the over-ingenious minds of pedagogues dealing with particular pupils. It will appear as part and parcel of the whole social evolution, and, in its more general features at least, as inevitable. Let us then ask after the main aspects of the social movement; and afterward turn to the school to find what witness it gives of effort to put itself in line. And since it is quite impossible to cover the whole ground, I shall for the most part confine myself in this chapter to one typical thing in the modern school movement—that which passes under the name of manual training—hoping, if the relation of that to changed social conditions appears, we shall be ready to concede the point as well regarding other educational innovations.

I make no apology for not dwelling at length upon the social changes in question. Those I shall mention are writ so large that he who runs may read. The change that comes first to mind, the one that overshadows and even controls all others, is the industrial one—the application of science resulting in the great inventions that have utilized the forces of nature on a vast and inexpensive scale: the growth of a world-wide market as the object of production, of vast manufacturing centers to supply this market, of cheap and rapid means of communication and distribution between all its parts. Even as to its feebler beginnings, this change is not much more than a century old; in many of its most important aspects it falls within the short span of those now living. One can hardly believe there has been a revolution in all history so rapid, so extensive, so complete. Through it the face of the earth is making over, even as to its physical forms; political boundaries are wiped out and moved about, as if they were indeed only lines on a paper map; population is hurriedly gathered into cities from the ends of the earth; habits of living are altered with startling abruptness and thoroughness; the search for the truths of nature is infinitely stimulated and facilitated, and their application to life made not only practicable, but commercially necessary. Even our moral and religious ideas and interests, the most conservative because the deepest-lying things in our nature, are profoundly affected. That this revolution should not affect education in some other than a formal and superficial fashion is inconceivable.

Back of the factory system lies the household and neighborhood system. Those of us who are here today need go back only one, two, or at most three generations, to find a time when the household was practically the center in which were carried on, or about which were clustered, all the typical forms of industrial occupation. The clothing worn was for the most part made in the house; the members of the household were usually familiar also with the shearing of the sheep, the carding and spinning of the wool, and the plying of the loom. Instead of pressing a button and flooding the house with electric light, the whole process of getting illumination was followed in its toilsome length from the killing of the animal and the trying of fat to the making of wicks and dipping of candles. The supply of flour, of lumber, of foods, of building materials, of household furniture, even of metal ware, of nails, hinges, hammers, etc., was produced in the immediate neighborhood, in shops which were constantly open to inspection and often centers of neighborhood congregation. The entire industrial process stood revealed, from the production on the farm of the raw materials till the finished article was actually put to use. Not only this, but practically every member of the household had his own share in the work. The children, as they gained in strength and capacity, were gradually initiated into the mysteries of the several processes. It was a matter of immediate and personal concern, even to the point of actual participation.

We cannot overlook the factors of discipline and of character-building involved in this kind of life: training in habits of order and of industry, and in the idea of responsibility, of obligation to do something, to produce something, in the world. There was always something which really needed to be done, and a real necessity that each member of the household should do his own part faithfully and in co-operation with others. Personalities which became effective in action were bred and tested in the medium of action. Again, we cannot overlook the importance for educational purposes of the close and intimate acquaintance got with nature at first hand, with real things and materials, with the actual processes of their manipulation, and the knowledge of their social necessities and uses. In all this there was continual training of observation, of ingenuity, constructive imagination, of logical thought, and of the sense of reality acquired through first-hand contact with actualities. The educative forces of the domestic spinning and weaving, of the sawmill, the gristmill, the cooper shop, and the blacksmith forge, were continuously operative.

No number of object-lessons, got up as object-lessons for the sake of giving information, can afford even the shadow of a substitute for acquaintance with the plants and animals of the farm and garden acquired through actual living among them and caring for them. No training of sense-organs in school, introduced for the sake of training, can begin to compete with the alertness and fulness of sense-life that comes through daily intimacy and interest in familiar occupations. Verbal memory can be trained in committing tasks, a certain discipline of the reasoning powers can be acquired through lessons in science and mathematics; but, after all, this is somewhat remote and shadowy compared with the training of attention and of judgment that is acquired in having to do things with a real motive behind and a real outcome ahead. At present, concentration of industry and division of labor have practically eliminated household and neighborhood occupations—at least for educational purposes. But it is useless to bemoan the departure of the good old days of children's modesty, reverence, and implicit obedience, if we expect merely by bemoaning and by exhortation to bring them back. It is radical conditions which have changed, and only an equally radical change in education suffices. We must recognize our compensations—the increase in toleration, in breadth of social judgment, the larger acquaintance with human nature, the sharpened alertness in reading signs of character and interpreting social situations, greater accuracy of adaptation to differing personalities, contact with greater commercial activities. These considerations mean much to the city-bred child of today. Yet there is a real problem: how shall we retain these advantages, and yet introduce into the school something representing the other side of life—occupations which exact personal responsibilities and which train the child in relation to the physical realities of life?

When we turn to the school, we find that one of the most

striking tendencies at present is toward the introduction of so-called manual training, shopwork, and the household arts—sewing and cooking.

This has not been done "on purpose," with a full consciousness that the school must now supply that factor of training formerly taken care of in the home, but rather by instinct, by experimenting and finding that such work takes a vital hold of pupils and gives them something which was not to be got in any other way. Consciousness of its real import is still so weak that the work is often done in a half-hearted, confused, and unrelated way. The reasons assigned to justify it are painfully inadequate or sometimes even positively wrong.

If we were to cross-examine even those who are most favorably disposed to the introduction of this work into our school system, we should, I imagine, generally find the main reasons to be that such work engages the full spontaneous interest and attention of the children. It keeps them alert and active, instead of passive and receptive; it makes them more useful, more capable, and hence more inclined to be helpful at home; it prepares them to some extent for the practical duties of later life—the girls to be more efficient house managers, if not actually cooks and seamstresses; the boys (were our educational system only adequately rounded out into trade schools) for their future vocations. I do not underestimate the worth of these reasons. Of those indicated

13

by the changed attitude of the children I shall indeed have something to say in the next chapter, when speaking directly of the relationship of the school to the child. But the point of view is, upon the whole, unnecessarily narrow. We must conceive of work in wood and metal, of weaving, sewing, and cooking, as methods of living and learning, not as distinct studies.

We must conceive of them in their social significance, as types of the processes by which society keeps itself going, as agencies for bringing home to the child some of the primal necessities of community life, and as ways in which these needs have been met by the growing insight and ingenuity of man; in short, as instrumentalities through which the school itself shall be made a genuine form of active community life, instead of a place set apart in which to learn lessons.

A society is a number of people held together because they are working along common lines, in a common spirit, and with reference to common aims. The common needs and aims demand a growing interchange of thought and growing unity of sympathetic feeling. The radical reason that the present school cannot organize itself as a natural social unit is because just this element of common and productive activity is absent. Upon the playground, in game and sport, social organization takes place spontaneously and inevitably. There is something to do, some activity to be carried on, requiring natural divisions of labor, selection of leaders

and followers, mutual co-operation and emulation. In the schoolroom the motive and the cement of social organization are alike
wanting. Upon the ethical side, the tragic weakness of the present
school is that it endeavors to prepare future members of the social
order in a medium in which the conditions of the social spirit are
eminently wanting.

The difference that appears when occupations are made the
articulating centers of school life is not easy to describe in words;
it is a difference in motive, of spirit and atmosphere. As one
enters a busy kitchen in which a group of children are actively
engaged in the preparation of food, the psychological difference,
the change from more or less passive and inert recipiency and
restraint to one of buoyant outgoing energy, is so obvious as fairly
to strike one in the face. Indeed, to those whose image of the
school is rigidly set the change is sure to give a shock. But the
change in the social attitude is equally marked. The mere absorb-
ing of facts and truths is so exclusively individual an affair that it
tends very naturally to pass into selfishness. There is no obvious
social motive for the acquirement of mere learning, there is no
clear social gain in success thereat. Indeed, almost the only
measure for success is a competitive one, in the bad sense of that
term—a comparison of results in the recitation or in the examination to see which child has succeeded in getting ahead of others
in storing up, in accumulating, the maximum of information. So

thoroughly is this the prevailing atmosphere that for one child to help another in his task has become a school crime. Where the school work consists in simply learning lessons, mutual assistance, instead of being the most natural form of co-operation and association, becomes a clandestine effort to relieve one's neighbor of his proper duties. Where active work is going on, all this is changed. Helping others, instead of being a form of charity which impoverishes the recipient, is simply an aid in setting free the powers and furthering the impulse of the one helped. A spirit of free communication, of interchange of ideas, suggestions, results, both successes and failures of previous experiences, becomes the dominating note of the recitation. So far as emulation enters in, it is in the comparison of individuals, not with regard to the quantity of information personally absorbed, but with reference to the quality of work done—the genuine community standard of value. In an informal but all the more pervasive way, the school life organizes itself on a social basis.

Within this organization is found the principle of school discipline or order. Of course, order is simply a thing which is relative to an end. If you have the end in view of forty or fifty children learning certain set lessons, to be recited to a teacher, your discipline must be devoted to securing that result. But if the end in view is the development of a spirit of social co-operation and community life, discipline must grow out of and be relative to such an aim. There is little of one sort of order where things are in process of construction; there is a certain disorder in any busy workshop; there is not silence; persons are not engaged in maintaining certain fixed physical postures; their arms are not folded; they are not holding their books thus and so. They are doing a variety of things, and there is the confusion, the bustle, that results from activity. But out of the occupation, out of doing things that are to produce results, and out of doing these in a social and co-operative way, there is born a discipline of its own kind and type. Our whole conception of school discipline changes when we get this point of view. In critical moments we all realize that the only discipline that stands by us, the only training that becomes intuition, is that got through life itself. That we learn from experience, and from books or the sayings of others *only* as they are related to experience, are not mere phrases. But the school has been so set apart, so isolated from the ordinary conditions and motives of life, that the place where children are sent for discipline is the one place in the world where it is most difficult to get experience—the mother of all discipline worth the name. It is only when a narrow and fixed image of traditional school discipline dominates that one is in any danger of overlooking that deeper and infinitely wider discipline that comes from having a part to do in constructive work, in contributing to a result which, social in spirit, is none the less obvious and tangible in form—

and hence in a form with reference to which responsibility may be exacted and accurate judgment passed.

The great thing to keep in mind, then, regarding the introduction into the school of various forms of active occupation, is that through them the entire spirit of the school is renewed. It has a chance to affiliate itself with life, to become the child's habitat, where he learns through directed living, instead of being only a place to learn lessons having an abstract and remote reference to some possible living to be done in the future. It gets a chance to be a miniature community, an embryonic society. This is the fundamental fact, and from this arise continuous and orderly streams of instruction. Under the industrial régime described, the child, after all, shared in the work, not for the sake of the sharing, but for the sake of the product. The educational results secured were real, yet incidental and dependent. But in the school the typical occupations followed are freed from all economic stress. The aim is not the economic value of the products, but the development of social power and insight. It is this liberation from narrow utilities, this openness to the possibilities of the human spirit, that makes these practical activities in the school allies of art and centers of science and history.

The unity of all the sciences is found in geography. The significance of geography is that it presents the earth as the enduring home of the occupations of man. The world without its relationship to human activity is less than a world. Human industry and achievement, apart from their roots in the earth, are not even a sentiment, hardly a name. The earth is the final source of all man's food. It is his continual shelter and protection, the raw material of all his activities, and the home to whose humanizing and idealizing all his achievement returns. It is the great field, the great mine, the great source of the energies of heat, light, and electricity; the great scene of ocean, stream, mountain, and plain, of which all our agriculture and mining and lumbering, all our manufacturing and distributing agencies, are but the partial elements and factors. It is through occupations determined by this environment that mankind has made its historical and political progress. It is through these occupations that the intellectual and emotional interpretation of nature has been developed. It is through what we do in and with the world that we read its meaning and measure its value.

In educational terms, this means that these occupations in the school shall not be mere practical devices or modes of routine employment, the gaining of better technical skill as cooks, seamstresses, or carpenters, but active centers of scientific insight into natural materials and processes, points of departure whence children shall be led out into a realization of the historic development of man. The actual significance of this can be told better through one illustration taken from actual school work than by general discourse.

There is nothing which strikes more oddly upon the average

intelligent visitor than to see boys as well as girls of ten, twelve, and thirteen years of age engaged in sewing and weaving. If we look at this from the standpoint of preparation of the boys for sewing on buttons and making patches, we get a narrow and utilitarian conception—a basis that hardly justifies giving prominence to this sort of work in the school. But if we look at it from another side, we find that this work gives the point of departure from which the child can trace and follow the progress of mankind in history, getting an insight also into the materials used and the mechanical principles involved. In connection with these occupations the historic development of man is recapitulated. For example, the children are first given the raw material—the flax, the cotton plant, the wool as it comes from the back of the sheep (if we could take them to the place where the sheep are sheared, so much the better). Then a study is made of these materials from the standpoint of their adaptation to the uses to which they may be put. For instance, a comparison of the cotton fiber with wool fiber is made. I did not know, until the children told me, that the reason for the late development of the cotton industry as compared with the woolen is that the cotton fiber is so very difficult to free by hand from the seeds. The children in one group worked thirty minutes freeing cotton fibers from the boll and seeds, and succeeded in getting out less than one ounce. They could easily believe that one person could gin only one pound a day by hand, and could understand why their ancestors wore woolen instead of cotton clothing. Among other things discovered as affecting their relative utilities was the shortness of the cotton fiber as compared with that of wool, the former averaging, say, one-third of an inch in length, while the latter run to three inches in length; also that the fibers of cotton are smooth and do not cling together, while the wool has a certain roughness which makes the fibers stick, thus assisting the spinning. The children worked this out for themselves with the actual material, aided by questions and suggestions from the teacher.

They then followed the processes necessary for working the fibers up into cloth. They reinvented the first frame for carding the wool—a couple of boards with sharp pins in them for scratching it out. They redevised the simplest process for spinning the wool—a pierced stone or some other weight through which the wool is passed, and which as it is twirled draws out the fiber; next the top, which was spun on the floor, while the children kept the wool in their hands until it was gradually drawn out and wound upon it. Then the children are introduced to the invention next in historic order, working it out experimentally, thus seeing its necessity, and tracing its effects, not only upon that particular industry, but upon modes of social life—in this way passing in review the entire process up to the present complete loom, and all that goes with the application of science in the use of our present available powers. I need not speak of the science involved in this—the study of the fibers, of geographical features, the conditions under which raw materials are grown, the great centers of manufacture and distribution, the physics involved in the machinery of production; nor, again, of the historical side—the influence which these inventions have had upon humanity. You can concentrate the history of all mankind into the evolution of the flax, cotton, and wool fibers into clothing. I do not mean that this is the only, or the best, center. But it is true that certain very real and important avenues to the consideration of the history of the race are thus opened—that the mind is introduced to much more fundamental and controlling influences than appear in the political and chronological records that usually pass for history.

Now, what is true of this one instance of fibers used in fabrics (and, of course, I have only spoken of one or two elementary phases of that) is true in its measure of every material used in every occupation, and of the processes employed. The occupation supplies the child with a genuine motive; it gives him experience at first hand; it brings him into contact with realities. It does all this, but in addition it is liberalized throughout by translation into its historic and social values and scientific equivalencies. With the growth of the child's mind in power and knowledge it ceases to be a pleasant occupation merely and becomes more and more a medium, an instrument, an organ of understanding—and is thereby transformed.

This, in turn, has its bearing upon the teaching of science.

Under present conditions, all activity, to be successful, has to be directed somewhere and somehow by the scientific expert—it is a case of applied science. This connection should determine its place in education. It is not only that the occupations, the so-called manual or industrial work in the school, give the opportunity for the introduction of science which illuminates them, which makes them material, freighted with meaning, instead of being mere devices of hand and eye; but that the scientific insight thus gained becomes an indispensable instrument of free and active participation in modern social life. Plato somewhere speaks of the slave as one who in his actions does not express his own ideas, but those of some other man. It is our social problem now, even more urgent than in the time of Plato, that method, purpose, understanding, shall exist in the consciousness of the one who does the work, that his activity shall have meaning to himself.

When occupations in the school are conceived in this broad and generous way, I can only stand lost in wonder at the objections so often heard, that such occupations are out of place in the school because they are materialistic, utilitarian, or even menial in their tendency. It sometimes seems to me that those who make these objections must live in quite another world. The world in which most of us live is a world in which everyone has a calling and occupation, something to do. Some are managers and others are subordinates. But the great thing for one as for the other is that each shall have had the education which enables him to see within his daily work all there is in it of large and human significance. How many of the employed are today mere appendages to the machines which they operate! This may be due in part to the machine itself or the régime which lays so much stress upon the products of the machine; but it is certainly due in large part to the fact that the worker has had no opportunity to develop his imagination and his sympathetic insight as to the social and scientific values found in his work. At present, the impulses which lie at the basis of the industrial system are either practically neglected or positively distorted during the school period. Until the instincts of construction and production are systematically laid hold of in the years of childhood and youth, until they are trained in social directions, enriched by historical interpretation, controlled and illuminated by scientific methods, we certainly are in no position even to locate the source of our economic evils, much less to deal with them effectively.

If we go back a few centuries, we find a practical monopoly of learning. The term *possession* of learning is, indeed, a happy one. Learning was a class matter. This was a necessary result of social conditions. There were not in existence any means by which the multitude could possibly have access to intellectual resources. These were stored up and hidden away in manuscripts. Of these there were at best only a few, and it required long and toilsome preparation to be able to do anything with them. A high-priest-hood of learning, which guarded the treasury of truth and which doled it out to the masses under severe restrictions, was the inevitable expression of these conditions. But, as a direct result of the industrial revolution of which we have been speaking, this has been changed. Printing was invented; it was made commercial. Books, magazines, papers were multiplied and cheapened. As a result of the locomotive and telegraph, frequent, rapid, and cheap intercommunication by mails and electricity was called into being. Travel has been rendered easy; freedom of movement, with its accompanying exchange of ideas, indefinitely facilitated. The result has been an intellectual revolution. Learning has been put into circulation. While there still is, and probably always will be, a particular class having the special business of inquiry in hand, a distinctively learned class is henceforth out of the question. It is an anachronism. Knowledge is no longer an immobile solid; it has been liquefied. It is actively moving in all the currents of society itself.

It is easy to see that this revolution, as regards the materials of knowledge, carries with it a marked change in the attitude of the individual. Stimuli of an intellectual sort pour in upon us in all kinds of ways. The merely intellectual life, the life of scholarship and of learning, thus gets a very altered value. Academic and scholastic, instead of being titles of honor, are becoming terms of reproach.

But all this means a necessary change in the attitude of the school, one of which we are as yet far from realizing the full force. Our school methods, and to a very considerable extent our curriculum, are inherited from the period when learning and command of certain symbols, affording as they did the only access to learning, were all-important. The ideals of this period are still largely in control, even where the outward methods and studies have been changed. We sometimes hear the introduction of manual training, art, and science into the elementary, and even the secondary, schools deprecated on the ground that they tend toward the production of specialists—that they detract from our present scheme of generous, liberal culture. The point of this objection would be ludicrous if it were not often so effective as to make it tragic. It is our present education which is highly specialized, one-sided, and narrow. It is an education dominated almost entirely by the mediaeval conception of learning. It is something which appeals for the most part simply to the intellectual aspect of our natures, our desire to learn, to accumulate information, and to get control of the symbols of learning; not to our impulses and tendencies to make, to do, to create, to produce, whether in the form of utility or of art. The very fact that manual training, art, and science are objected to as technical, as tending toward mere specialism, is of itself as good testinmony as could be offered to the specialized aim which controls current education. Unless education had been virtually identified with the exclusively intellectual pursuits, with learning as such, all these materials and methods would be welcome, would be greeted with the utmost hospitality.

While training for the profession of learning is regarded as the type of culture, or a liberal education, the training of a mechanic, a musician, a lawyer, a doctor, a farmer, a merchant, or a railroad manager is regarded as purely technical and professional. The result is that which we see about us everywhere—the division into "cultured" people and "workers," the separation of theory and practice. Hardly 1 per cent of the entire school population ever attains to what we call higher education; only 5 per cent to the grade of our high school; while much more than half leave on or before the completion of the fifth year of the elementary grade. The simple facts of the case are that in the great majority of human beings the distinctively intellectual interest is not dominant. They have the so-called practical impulse and disposition. In many of those in whom by nature intellectual interest is strong, social conditions prevent its adequate realization. Consequently by far the larger number of pupils leave school as soon as they have acquired the rudiments of learning, as soon as they have enough of the symbols of reading, writing, and calculating

27

to be of practical use to them in getting a living. While our educational leaders are talking of culture, the development of personality, etc., as the end and aim of education, the great majority of those who pass under the tuition of the school regard it only as a narrowly practical tool with which to get bread and butter enough to eke out a restricted life. If we were to conceive our educational end and aim in a less exclusive way, if we were to introduce into educational processes the activities which appeal to those whose dominant interest is to do and to make, we should find the hold of the school upon its members to be more vital, more prolonged, containing more of culture.

But why should I make this labored presentation? The obvious fact is that our social life has undergone a thorough and radical change. If our education is to have any meaning for life, it must pass through an equally complete transformation. This transformation is not something to appear suddenly, to be executed in a day by conscious purpose. It is already in progress. Those modifications of our school system which often appear (even to those most actively concerned with them, to say nothing of their spectators) to be mere changes of detail, mere improvement within the school mechanism, are in reality signs and evidences of evolution. The introduction of active occupations, of nature-study, of elementary science, of art, of history; the relegation of the merely symbolic and formal to a secondary position; the change in the moral school atmosphere, in the relation of pupils and teachers—of discipline; the introduction of more active, expressive, and self-directing factors—all these are not mere accidents, they are necessities of the larger social evolution. It remains but to organize all these factors, to appreciate them in their fulness of meaning, and to put the ideas and ideals involved into complete, uncompromising possession of our school system. To do this means to make each one of our schools an embryonic community life, active with types of occupations that reflect the life of the larger society and permeated throughout with the spirit of art, history, and science. When the school introduces and trains each child of society into membership within such a little community, saturating him with the spirit of service, and providing him with the instruments of effective self-direction, we shall have the deepest and best guaranty of a larger society which is worthy, lovely, and harmonious.

II
The School and the Life of the Child

In the last chapter I tried to set forth the relationship between the school and the larger life of the community, and the necessity for certain changes in the methods and materials of school work, that it might be better adapted to present social needs.

Here I wish to look at the matter from the other side and consider the relationship of the school to the life and development of the children in the school. As it is difficult to connect general principles with such thoroughly concrete things as little children, I have taken the liberty of introducing a great deal of illustrative matter from the work of the University Elementary School, that in some measure you may appreciate the way in which the ideas presented work themselves out in actual practice.

Some few years ago I was looking about the school supply stores in the city, trying to find desks and chairs which seemed thoroughly suitable from all points of view—artistic, hygienic, and educational—to the needs of the children. We had a great deal of difficulty in finding what we needed, and finally one dealer, more intelligent than the rest, made this remark: "I am afraid we have not what you want. You want something at which the children may work; these are all for listening." That tells the story of the traditional education. Just as the biologist can take a bone or two and reconstruct the whole animal, so, if we put before the mind's eye the ordinary schoolroom, with its rows of ugly desks placed in geometrical order, crowded together so that there shall be as little moving room as possible, desks almost all of the same size, with just space enough to hold books, pencils, and paper, and add a table, some chairs, the bare walls, and possibly a few pictures, we can reconstruct the only educational activity that can possibly go on in such a place. It is all made "for listening"—because simply studying lessons out of a book is only another kind of listening; it marks the dependency of one mind upon another. The attitude of listening means, comparatively speaking, passivity, absorption; that there are certain ready-made materials which are there, which have been prepared by the school superintendent, the board, the teacher, and of which the child is to take in as much as possible in the least possible time.

There is very little place in the traditional schoolroom for the child to work. The workshop, the laboratory, the materials, the tools with which the child may construct, create, and actively inquire, and even the requisite space, have been for the most part lacking. The things that have to do with these processes have not even a definitely recognized place in education. They are what the educational authorities who write editorials in the daily papers generally term "fads" and "frills." A lady told me yesterday that she had been visiting different schools trying to find one where activity on the part of the children preceded the giving of information on the part of the teacher, or where the children had some motive for demanding the information. She visited, she said, twenty-four different schools before she found her first instance. I may add that that was not in this city.

Another thing that is suggested by these schoolrooms, with their set desks, is that everything is arranged for handling as large numbers of children as possible; for dealing with children *en masse*, as an aggregate of units; involving, again, that they be treated passively. The moment children act they individualize themselves; they cease to be a mass and become the intensely distinctive beings that we are acquainted with out of school, in the home, the family, on the playground, and in the neighborhood.

On the same basis is explicable the uniformity of method and curriculum. If everything is on a "listening" basis, you can have uniformity of material and method. The ear, and the book which reflects the ear, constitute the medium which is alike for all. There is next to no opportunity for adjustment to varying capacities and demands. There is a certain amount—a fixed quantity— of ready-made results and accomplishments to be acquired by all children alike in a given time. It is in response to this demand that the curriculum has been developed from the elementary school up through the college. There is just so much desirable knowledge, and there are just so many needed technical accomplishments in the world. Then comes the mathematical problem of dividing this by the six, twelve, or sixteen years of school life. Now give the children every year just the proportionate fraction of the total, and by the time they have finished they will have mastered the whole. By covering so much ground during this hour or day or week or year, everything comes out with perfect evenness at the end—provided the children have not forgotten what they have previously learned. The outcome of all this is Matthew Arnold's report of the statement, proudly made to him by an educational authority in France, that so many thousands of children were studying at a given hour, say eleven o'clock, just such a lesson in geography; and in one of our own western cities this proud boast used to be repeated to successive visitors by its superintendent.

I may have exaggerated somewhat in order to make plain the typical points of the old education: its passivity of attitude, its mechanical massing of children, its uniformity of curriculum and method. It may be summed up by stating that the center of gravity is outside the child. It is in the teacher, the textbook, anywhere and everywhere you please except in the immediate instincts and activities of the child himself. On that basis there is not much to be said about the *life* of the child. A good deal might be said about the studying of the child, but the school is not the place where the child *lives*. Now the change which is coming into our education is the shifting of the center of gravity. It is a change, a revolution, not unlike that introduced by Copernicus when the astronomical center shifted from the earth to the sun. In this case the child becomes the sun about which the appliances of education revolve; he is the center about which they are organized.

If we take an example from an ideal home, where the parent is intelligent enough to recognize what is best for the child, and is able to supply what is needed, we find the child learning through the social converse and constitution of the family. There are certain points of interest and value to him in the conversation carried on: statements are made, inquiries arise, topics are discussed, and the child continually learns. He states his experiences, his misconceptions are corrected. Again the child participates in the household occupations, and thereby gets habits of industry, order, and regard for the rights and ideas of others, and the fundamental habit of subordinating his activities to the general interest of the household. Participation in these household tasks becomes an opportunity for gaining knowledge. The ideal home would naturally have a workshop where the child could work out his constructive instincts. It would have a miniature laboratory in which his inquiries could be directed. The life of the child would extend out of doors to the garden, surrounding fields, and forests. He would have his excursions, his walks and talks, in which the larger world out of doors would open to him.

Now, if we organize and generalize all of this, we have the ideal school. There is no mystery about it, no wonderful discovery of pedagogy or educational theory. It is simply a question of doing systematically and in a large, intelligent, and competent way what for various reasons can be done in most households only in a comparatively meager and haphazard manner. In the first place, the ideal home has to be enlarged. The child must be brought into contact with more grown people and with more children in order that there may be the freest and richest social life. Moreover, the occupations and relationships of the home environment are not specially selected for the growth of the child; the main object is something else, and what the child can get out of them is incidental. Hence the need of a school. In this school the life of the child becomes the all-controlling aim. All the media necessary to further the growth of the child center there. Learning? certainly, but living primarily, and learning through and in relation to this living. When we take the life of the child centered and organized in this way, we do not find that he is first of all a listening being; quite the contrary.

The statement so frequently made that education means "drawing out" is excellent, if we mean simply to contrast it with the process of pouring in. But, after all, it is difficult to connect the idea of drawing out with the ordinary doings of the child of three, four, seven, or eight years of age. He is already running over, spilling over, with activities of all kinds. He is not a purely latent being whom the adult has to approach with great caution and skill in order gradually to draw out some hidden germ of activity. The child is already intensely active, and the question of education is the question of taking hold of his activities, of giving them direction. Through direction, through organized use, they tend toward valuable results, instead of scattering or being left to merely impulsive expression.

If we keep this before us, the difficulty I find uppermost in the minds of many people regarding what is termed the new education is not so much solved as dissolved; it disappears. A question often asked is: If you begin with the child's ideas, impulses, and interests, all so crude, so random and scattering, so little refined or spiritualized, how is he going to get the necessary discipline, culture, and information? If there were no way open to us except to excite and indulge these impulses of the child, the question might well be asked. We should either have to ignore and repress the activities or else to humor them. But if we have organization of equipment and of materials, there is another path open to us. We can direct the child's activities, giving them exercise along certain lines, and can thus lead up to the goal which logically stands at the end of the paths followed.

"If wishes were horses, beggars would ride." Since they are not, since really to satisfy an impulse or interest means to work it out, and working it out involves running up against obstacles, becoming acquainted with materials, exercising ingenuity, patience, persistence, alertness, it of necessity involves discipline—ordering of power—and supplies knowledge. Take the example of the little child who wants to make a box. If he stops short with the imagination or wish, he certainly will not get discipline. But when he attempts to realize his impulse, it is a question of making his idea definite, making it into a plan, of taking the right kind of wood, measuring the parts needed, giving them the necessary proportions, etc. There is involved the preparation of materials, the sawing, planing, the sandpapering, making all the edges and corners to fit. Knowledge of tools and processes is inevitable. If the child realizes his instinct and makes the box, there is plenty of opportunity to gain discipline and perseverance, to exercise effort in overcoming obstacles, and to attain as well a great deal of information.

So undoubtedly the little child who thinks he would like to cook has little idea of what it means or costs, or what it requires. It is simply a desire to "mess around," perhaps to imitate the activities of older people. And it is doubtless possible to let ourselves down to that level and simply humor that interest. But here, too, if the impulse is exercised, utilized, it runs up against the actual world of hard conditions, to which it must accommodate itself; and there again come in the factors of discipline and knowledge. One of the children became impatient, recently, at having to work things out by a long method of experimentation, and said "Why do we bother with this? Let's follow a recipe in a cookbook." The teacher asked the children where the recipe came from, and the conversation showed that if they simply followed this they would not understand the reasons for what they were doing. They were then quite willing to go on with the experimental work. To follow that work will, indeed, give an illustration of just the point in question. Their occupation happened that day to be the cooking of eggs, as making a transition from the cooking of vegetables to that of meats. In order to get a basis of comparison they first summarized the constituent food elements in the vegetables and made a preliminary comparison with those found in meat. Thus they found that the woody fiber or cellulose in vegetables corresponded to the connective tissue in meat, giving the element of form and structure. They found that starch and starchy products were characteristic of the vegetables, that mineral salts were found in both alike, and that there was fat in both—a small quantity in vegetable food and a large amount in animal. They were prepared then to take up the study of albumen as the characteristic feature of animal food, corresponding to starch in the vegetables, and were ready to consider the conditions requisite for the proper treatment of albumen—the eggs serving as the material of experiment.

They experimented first by taking water at various temperatures, finding out when it was scalding, simmering, and boiling hot, and ascertained the effect of the various degrees of temperature on the white of the egg. That worked out, they were prepared, not simply to cook eggs, but to understand the principle involved in the cooking of eggs. I do not wish to lose sight of the universal in the particular incident. For the child simply to desire to cook an egg, and accordingly drop it in water for three minutes, and take it out when he is told, is not educative. But for the child to realize his own impulse by recognizing the facts, materials, and conditions involved, and then to regulate his impulse through that recognition, is educative. This is the difference, upon which I wish to insist, between exciting or indulging an interest and realizing it through its direction.

Another instinct of the child is the use of pencil and paper. All children like to express themselves through the medium of form and color. If you simply indulge this interest by letting the child go on indefinitely, there is no growth that is more than accidental. But let the child first express his impulse, and then through criticism, question, and suggestion bring him to consciousness of what he has done, and what he needs to do, and the result is quite different. Here, for example (Fig. 1), is the work of a seven-year-old child. It is not average work, it is the best work done among the little children, but it illustrates the particular principle of which I have been speaking. They had been talking about the primitive conditions of social life when people lived in caves. The child's idea of that found expression in this way: the cave is neatly set up on the hillside in an impossible way. You see the conventional tree of childhood—a vertical line with horizontal branches on each side. If the child had been allowed to go on repeating this sort of thing day by day, he would be indulging his instinct rather than exercising it. But the child was now asked to

Fig. 1. Drawing of a Cave and Trees

look closely at trees, to compare those seen with the one drawn, to examine more closely and consciously into the conditions of his work. Then he drew trees from observation.

Finally he drew again from combined observation, memory, and imagination. He made again a free illustration, expressing his own imaginative thought, but controlled by detailed study of actual trees. The result was a scene representing a bit of forest (Fig. 2); so far as it goes, it seems to me to have as much poetic feeling as the work of an adult, while at the same time its trees are, in their proportions, possible ones, not mere symbols.

If we roughly classify the impulses which are available in the school, we may group them under four heads. There is the social instinct of the children as shown in conversation, personal intercourse, and communication. We all know how self-centered the little child is at the age of four or five. If any new subject is brought up, if he says anything at all, it is: "I have seen that"; or, "My papa or mamma told me about that." His horizon is not large; an experience must come immediately home to him, if he is to be sufficiently interested to relate it to others and seek theirs in return. And yet the egoistic and limited interest of little children is in this manner capable of infinite expansion. The language instinct is the simplest form of the social expression of the child. Hence it is a great, perhaps the greatest of all, educational resources.

Then there is the instinct of making—the constructive impulse. The child's impulse to do finds expression first in play, in movement, gesture, and make-believe, becomes more definite, and seeks outlet in shaping materials into tangible forms and permanent embodiment. The child has not much instinct for abstract inquiry. The instinct of investigation seems to grow out of the combination of the constructive impulse with the conversational. There is no distinction between experimental science for little children and the work done in the carpenter shop. Such work as they can do in physics or chemistry is not for the purpose of making technical generalizations or even arriving at abstract truths. Children simply like to do things and watch to see what will happen. But this can be taken advantage of, can be directed into ways where it gives results of value, as well as be allowed to go on at random.

And so the expressive impulse of the children, the art instinct, grows also out of the communicating and constructive instincts. It is their refinement and full manifestation. Make the construction adequate, make it full, free, and flexible, give it a social motive, something to tell, and you have a work of art. Take one illustration of this in connection with the textile work—sewing and weaving. The children made a primitive loom in the shop; here the constructive instinct was appealed to. Then they wished to do something with this loom, to make something. It was the

FIG. 2. DRAWING OF A FOREST

type of the Indian loom, and they were shown blankets woven by the Indians. Each child made a design kindred in idea to those of the Navajo blankets, and the one which seemed best adapted to the work in hand was selected. The technical resources were limited, but the coloring and form were worked out by the children. Examination of the work of the twelve-year-olds shows that it took patience, thoroughness, and perseverance. It involved not merely discipline and information of both a historical sort and the elements of technical design, but also something of the spirit of art in adequately conveying an idea.

One more instance of the connection of the art side with the constructive side: The children had been studying primitive spinning and carding, when one of them, twelve years of age, made a picture of one of the children spinning (Fig. 3). Here is still another piece of work which is not quite average; it is better than the average. It is an illustration of two hands and the drawing out of the wool to get it ready for spinning (Fig. 4). This was done by a child eleven years of age. But, upon the whole, with the younger children especially, the art impulse is connected mainly with the social instinct—the desire to tell, to represent.

Now, keeping in mind these fourfold interests—the interest in conversation, or communication; in inquiry, or finding out things; in making things, or construction; and in artistic expression—we may say they are the natural resources, the uninvested capital, upon the exercise of which depends the active growth of the child. I wish to give one or two illustrations, the first from the work of children seven years of age. It illustrates in a way the dominant desire of the children to talk, particularly about folks and of things in relation to folks. If you observe little children, you will find they are interested in the world of things mainly in its connection with people, as a background and medium of human concerns. Many anthropologists have told us there are certain identities in the child interests with those of primitive life. There is a sort of natural recurrence of the child mind to the typical activities of primitive peoples; witness the hut which the boy likes to build in the yard, playing hunt, with bows, arrows, spears, and so on. Again the question comes: What are we to do with this interest—are we to ignore it, or just excite and draw it out? Or shall we get hold of it and direct it to something ahead, something better? Some of the work that has been planned for our seven-year-old children has the latter end in view—to utilize this interest so that it shall become a means of seeing the progress of the human race. The children begin by imagining present conditions taken away until they are in contact with nature at first hand. That takes them back to a hunting people, to a people living in caves or trees and getting a precarious subsistence by hunting and fishing. They imagine as far as possible the various natural physical conditions adapted to that sort of life; say, a hilly,

Fig. 3. Drawing of a Girl Spinning

FIG. 4. DRAWING OF HANDS SPINNING

woody slope, near mountains, and a river where fish would be abundant. Then they go on in imagination through the hunting to the semi-agricultural stage, and through the nomadic to the settled agricultural stage. The point I wish to make is that there is abundant opportunity thus given for actual study, for inquiry which results in gaining information. So, while the instinct primarily appeals to the social side, the interest of the child in people and their doings is carried on into the larger world of reality. For example, the children had some idea of primitive weapons, of the stone arrowhead, etc. That provided occasion for the testing of materials as regards their friability, their shape, texture, etc., resulting in a lesson in mineralogy, as they examined the different stones to find which was best suited to the purpose. The discussion of the iron age supplied a demand for the construction of a smelting oven made out of clay and of considerable size. As the children did not get their drafts right at first, the mouth of the furnace not being in proper relation to the vent as to size and position, instruction in the principles of combustion, the nature of drafts and of fuel, was required. Yet the instruction was not given ready-made; it was first needed, and then arrived at experimentally. Then the children took some material, such as copper, and went through a series of experiments, fusing it, working it into objects; and the same experiments were made with lead and other metals. This work has been also a continuous course in geography, since the children have had to imagine and work out the various physical conditions necessary to the different forms of social life implied. What would be the physical conditions appropriate to pastoral life? to the beginning of agriculture? to fishing? What would be the natural method of exchange between these peoples? Having worked out such points in conversation, they have afterward represented them in maps and sand-molding. Thus they have gained ideas of the various forms of the configuration of the earth, and at the same time have seen them in their relation to human activity, so that they are not simply external facts, but are fused and welded with social conceptions regarding the life and progress of humanity. The result, to my mind, justifies completely the conviction that children, in a year of such work (of five hours a week altogether), get infinitely more acquaintance with facts of science, geography, and anthropology than they get where information is the professed end and object, where they are simply set to learning facts in fixed lessons. As to discipline, they get more training of attention, more power of interpretation, of drawing inferences, of acute observation and continuous reflection, than if they were put to working out arbitrary problems simply for the sake of discipline.

I should like at this point to refer to the recitation. We all know what it has been—a place where the child shows off to the teacher and the other children the amount of information he has succeeded in assimilating from the textbook. From this other standpoint the recitation becomes pre-eminently a social meeting-place; it is to the school what the spontaneous conversation is at home, excepting that it is more organized, following definite lines. The recitation becomes the social clearing-house, where experiences and ideas are exchanged and subjected to criticism, where misconceptions are corrected, and new lines of thought and inquiry are set up.

This change of the recitation, from an examination of knowledge already acquired to the free play of the children's communicative instinct, affects and modifies all the language work of the school. Under the old régime it was unquestionably a most serious problem to give the children a full and free use of language. The reason was obvious. The natural motive for language was seldom offered. In the pedagogical textbooks language is defined as the medium of expressing thought. It becomes that, more or less, to adults with trained minds, but it hardly needs to be said that language is primarily a social thing, a means by which we give our experiences to others and get theirs again in return. When it is taken away from its natural purpose, it is no wonder that it becomes a complex and difficult problem to teach language. Think of the absurdity of having to teach language as a thing by itself. If there is anything the child will do before he goes to school, it is to talk of the things that interest him. But when there are no vital interests appealed to in the school, when language is used simply for the repetition of lessons, it is not surprising that one of the chief difficulties of school work has come to be instruction in the mother-tongue. Since the language taught is unnatural, not growing out of the real desire to communicate vital impressions and convictions, the freedom of children in its use gradually disappears, until finally the high-school teacher has to invent all kinds of devices to assist in getting any spontaneous and full use of speech. Moreover, when the language instinct is appealed to in a social way, there is a continual contact with reality. The result is that the child always has something in his mind to talk about, he has something to say; he has a thought to express, and a thought is not a thought unless it is one's own. On the traditional method, the child must say something that he has merely learned. There is all the difference in the world between having something to say and having to say something. The child who has a variety of materials and facts wants to talk about them, and his language becomes more refined and full, because it is controlled and informed by realities. Reading and writing, as well as the oral use of language, may be taught on this basis. It can be done in a *related* way, as the outgrowth of the child's social desire to recount his experiences and get in return the experiences of others, directed always through contact with the facts and forces which determine the truth communicated.

I do not have space to speak of the work of the older children, where the original crude instincts of construction and communication have been developed into something like scientifically directed inquiry, but I will give an illustration of the use of language following upon this experimental work. The work was on the basis of a simple experiment of the commonest sort, gradually leading the children out into geological and geographical study. The sentences that I am going to cite seem to me poetic as well as "scientific." "A long time ago when the earth was new, when it was lava, there was no water on the earth, and there was steam all round the earth up in the air, as there were many gases in the air. One of them was carbon dioxide. The steam became clouds, because the earth began to cool off, and after a while it began to rain, and the water came down and dissolved the carbon dioxide from the air." There is a good deal more science in that than probably would be apparent at the outset. It represents some three months of work on the part of the child. The children kept daily and weekly records, but this is part of the summing up of the quarter's work. I call this language poetic, because the child has a clear image and has a personal feeling for the realities imaged. I extract sentences from two other records to illustrate further the vivid use of language when there is a vivid experience back of it. "When the earth was cold enough to condense, the water, with the help of carbon dioxide, *pulled* the calcium out of the rocks into a large body of water where the little animals could get it." The other reads as follows: "When the earth cooled, calcium was in the rocks. Then the carbon dioxide and water united and formed a solution, and, as it ran, it tore out the calcium and carried it on to the sea, where there were little animals who took it out of solution." The use of such words as "pulled" and "tore" in connection with the process of chemical combination evidences a personal realization which compels its own appropriate expression.

If I had not taken so much space in my other illustrations, I should like to show how, beginning with very simple material things, the children are led on to larger fields of investigation and to the intellectual discipline that is the accompaniment of such research. I will simply refer to the experiment in which the work began. It consisted in making precipitated chalk, used for polishing metals. The children, with simple apparatus—a tumbler, lime water, and a glass tube—precipitated the calcium carbonate out of the water; and from this beginning went on to a study of the processes by which rocks of various sorts, igneous, sedimentary, etc., had been formed on the surface of the earth and the places they occupy; then to points in the geography of the United States, Hawaii, and Puerto Rico; to the effects of these various bodies of rock, in their various configurations, upon the human occupations; so that this geological record finally rounded itself out into the life of man at the present time. The children saw and felt the connection between these geologic processes, taking place ages and ages ago, and the physical conditions determining the industrial occupations of today.

Of all the possibilities involved in the subject, "The School and the Life of the Child," I have selected but one, because I have found that it gives people more difficulty, is more of a stumbling-block, than any other. One may be ready to admit that it would be most desirable for the school to be a place in which the child should really live, and get a life-experience in which he should delight and find meaning for its own sake. But then we hear this inquiry: How, upon this basis, shall the child get the needed information; how shall he undergo the required discipline? Yes, it has come to this, that with many, if not most, people the normal processes of life appear to be incompatible with getting information and discipline. So I have tried to indicate, in a highly general and inadequate way (for only the school itself, in its daily operation, could give a detailed and worthy representation), how the problem works itself out—how it is possible to lay hold upon the rudimentary instincts of human nature, and, by supplying a proper medium, so to control their expression as not only to facilitate and enrich the growth of the individual child, but also to supply the same results, and far more, of technical information and discipline that have been the ideals of education in the past.

But although I have selected this especial way of approach (as a concession to the question almost universally raised), I am not willing to leave the matter in this more or less negative and explanatory condition. Life is the great thing after all; the life of the child at its time and in its measure no less than the life of the adult. Strange would it be, indeed, if intelligent and serious attention to what the child *now* needs and is capable of in the way of a rich, valuable, and expanded life should somehow conflict with the needs and possibilities of later, adult life. "Let us live with our children" certainly means, first of all, that our children shall live—not that they shall be hampered and stunted by being forced into all kinds of conditions, the most remote consideration of which is relevancy to the present life of the child. If we seek the kingdom of heaven, educationally, all other things shall be added unto us—which, being interpreted, is that if we identify ourselves with the real instincts and needs of childhood, and ask only after its fullest assertion and growth, the discipline and information and culture of adult life shall all come in their due season.

Speaking of culture reminds me that in a way I have been speaking only of the outside of the child's activity—only of the outward expression of his impulses toward saying, making, finding out, and creating. The real child, it hardly need be said, lives in the world of imaginative values and ideas which find only imperfect outward embodiment. We hear much nowadays about the cultivation of the child's "imagination." Then we undo much of our own talk and work by a belief that the imagination is some special part of the child that finds its satisfaction in some one particular direction—generally speaking, that of the unreal and make-believe, of the myth and made-up story. Why are we so hard of heart and so slow to believe? The imagination is the medium in which the child lives. To him there is everywhere and in everything which occupies his mind and activity at all a surplusage of value and significance. The question of the relation of the school to the child's life is at bottom simply this: Shall we ignore this native setting and tendency, dealing, not with the living child at all, but with the dead image we have erected, or shall we give it play and satisfaction? If we once believe in life and in the life of the child, then will all the occupations and uses spoken of, then will all history and science, become instruments of appeal and materials of culture to his imagination, and through that to the richness and the orderliness of his life. Where we now see only the outward doing and the outward product, there, behind all visible results, is the readjustment of mental attitude, the enlarged and sympathetic vision, the sense of growing power, and the willing ability to identify both insight and capacity with the interests of the world and man. Unless culture be a superficial polish, a veneering of mahogany over common wood, it surely is this—the growth of the imagination in flexibility, in scope, and in sympathy, till the life which the individual lives is informed with the life of nature and of society. When nature and society can live in the schoolroom, when the forms and tools of learning are subordinated to the substance of experience, then shall there be an opportunity for this identification, and culture shall be the democratic password.

III

Waste in Education

The first chapter dealt with the school in its social aspects, and the necessary readjustments that have to be made to render it effective in present social conditions. The second dealt with the school in relation to the growth of individual children. Now the third deals with the school as itself an institution, in relation both to society and to its own members—the children. It deals with the question of organization, because all waste is the result of the lack of it, the motive lying behind organization being promotion of economy and efficiency. This question is not one of the waste of money or the waste of things. These matters count; but the primary waste is that of human life, the life of the children while they are at school, and afterward because of inadequate and perverted preparation.

So, when we speak of organization, we are not to think simply of the externals; of that which goes by the name "school system" —the school board, the superintendent, and the building, the engaging and promotion of teachers, etc. These things enter in, but the fundamental organization is that of the school itself as a community of individuals, in its relations to other forms of social life. All waste is due to isolation. Organization is nothing but getting things into connection with one another, so that they work easily, flexibly, and fully. Therefore in speaking of this question of waste in education I desire to call your attention to the isolation of the various parts of the school system, to the lack of unity in the aims of education, to the lack of coherence in its studies and methods.

I have made a chart (I) which, while I speak of the isolations of the school system itself, may perhaps appeal to the eye and save a little time in verbal explanations. A paradoxical friend of mine says there is nothing so obscure as an illustration, and it is

PROFESSIONAL SCHOOLS

THE 19TH CENTURY
UTILITY

MEDIAEVAL
CULTURE

COLLEGE
SCHOOLS

UNIVERSITY
GRADUATE

MEDIAEVAL
CULTURE
DISCIPLINE

HIGH SCHOOL
OR ACADEMY

RENAISSANCE
CULTURE
DISCIPLINE

NORMAL

19TH CENTURY
UTILITY CULTURE

TECHNICAL SCHOOLS

19TH CENTURY
UTILITY

GRAMMAR OR
INTERMEDIATE SCHOOL

RENAISSANCE
CULTURE
DISCIPLINE

PRIMARY

16TH CENTURY
UTILITY

KINDERGARTEN

18TH CENTURY
MORAL

CONNECTING
CLASS

19TH CENTURY

CHART I

quite possible that my attempt to illustrate my point will simply prove the truth of his statement.

The blocks represent the various elements in the school system and are intended to indicate roughly the length of time given to each division, and also the overlapping, both in time and in subjects studied, of the individual parts of the system. With each block is given the historical conditions in which it arose and its ruling ideal.

The school system, upon the whole, has grown from the top down. During the Middle Ages it was essentially a cluster of professional schools—especially law and theology. Our present university comes down to us from the Middle Ages. I will not say that at present it is a mediaeval institution, but it had its roots in the Middle Ages, and it has not outlived all mediaeval traditions regarding learning.

The kindergarten, rising with the present century, was a union of the nursery and of the philosophy of Schelling; a wedding of the plays and games which the mother carried on with her children to Schelling's highly romantic and symbolic philosophy. The elements that came from the actual study of child life—the continuation of the nursery—have remained a life-bringing force in all education; the Schellingesque factors made an obstruction between it and the rest of the school system—brought about isolations.

The line drawn over the top indicates that there is a certain interaction between the kindergarten and the primary school; for, so far as the primary school remained in spirit foreign to the natural interests of child life, it was isolated from the kindergarten, so that it is a problem, at present, to introduce kindergarten methods into the primary school; the problem of the so-called connecting class. The difficulty is that the two are not one from the start. To get a connection the teacher has had to climb over the wall instead of entering in at the gate.

On the side of aims, the ideal of the kindergarten was the moral development of the children, rather than instruction or discipline; an ideal sometimes emphasized to the point of sentimentality. The primary school grew practically out of the popular movement of the sixteenth century, when, along with the invention of printing and the growth of commerce, it became a business necessity to know how to read, write, and figure. The aim was distinctly a practical one; it was utility; getting command of these tools, the symbols of learning, not for the sake of learning, but because they gave access to careers in life otherwise closed.

The division next to the primary school is the grammar school. The term is not much used in the West, but is common in the eastern states. It goes back to the time of the revival of learning —a little earlier perhaps than the conditions out of which the primary school originated, and, even when contemporaneous, having a different ideal. It had to do with the study of language in the higher sense; because, at the time of the Renaissance, Latin and Greek connected people with the culture of the past, with the Roman and Greek world. The classic languages were the only means of escape from the limitations of the Middle Ages. Thus there sprang up the prototype of the grammar school, more liberal than the university (so largely professional in character), for the purpose of putting into the hands of the people the key to the old learning, that men might see a world with a larger horizon. The object was primarily culture, secondarily discipline. It represented much more than the present grammar school. It was the liberal element in the college, which, extending downward, grew into the academy and the high school. Thus the secondary school is still in part just a lower college (having an even higher curriculum than the college of a few centuries ago) or a preparatory department to a college, and in part a rounding up of the utilities of the elementary school.

There appear then two products of the nineteenth century, the technical and normal schools. The schools of technology, engineering, etc., are, of course, mainly the development of nineteenth-century business conditions, as the primary school was the development of business conditions of the sixteenth century. The normal school arose because of the necessity for training teachers, with the idea partly of professional drill and partly that of culture.

Without going more into detail, we have some eight different parts of the school system as represented on the chart, all of which arose historically at different times, having different ideals in view, and consequently different methods. I do not wish to suggest that all of the isolation, all of the separation, that has existed in the past between the different parts of the school system still persists. One must, however, recognize that they have never yet been welded into one complete whole. The great problem in education on the administrative side is how to unite these different parts.

Consider the training schools for teachers—the normal schools. These occupy at present a somewhat anomalous position, intermediate between the high school and the college, requiring the high-school preparation, and covering a certain amount of college work. They are isolated from the higher subject-matter of scholarship, since, upon the whole, their object has been to train persons *how* to teach, rather than *what* to teach; while, if we go to the college, we find the other half of this isolation—learning *what* to teach, with almost a contempt for methods of teaching. The college is shut off from contact with children and youth. Its members, to a great extent, away from home and forgetting their own childhood, become eventually teachers with a large amount of subject-matter at command, and little knowledge of how this is related to the minds of those to whom it is to be taught. In this division between what to teach and how to teach, each side suffers from the separation.

It is interesting to follow out the interrelation between primary, grammar, and high schools. The elementary school has crowded up and taken many subjects previously studied in the old New England grammar school. The high school has pushed its subjects down. Latin and algebra have been put in the upper grades, so that the seventh and eighth grades are, after all, about all that is left of the old grammar school. They are a sort of amorphous composite, being partly a place where children go on learning what they already have learned (to read, write, and figure), and partly a place of preparation for the high school. The name in some parts of New England for these upper grades was "Intermediate School." The term was a happy one; the work was simply intermediate between something that had been and something that was going to be, having no special meaning on its own account.

Just as the parts are separated, so do the ideals differ—moral development, practical utility, general culture, discipline, and professional training. These aims are each especially represented in some distinct part of the system of education; and, with the growing interaction of the parts, each is supposed to afford a certain amount of culture, discipline, and utility. But the lack of fundamental unity is witnessed in the fact that one study is still considered good for discipline, and another for culture; some parts of arithmetic, for example, for discipline and others for use; literature for culture; grammar for discipline; geography partly for utility, partly for culture; and so on. The unity of education is dissipated, and the studies become centrifugal; so much of this study to secure this end, so much of that to secure another, until the whole becomes a sheer compromise and patchwork between contending aims and disparate studies. The great problem in education on the administrative side is to secure the unity of the whole, in the place of a sequence of more or less unrelated and overlapping parts, and thus to reduce the waste arising from friction, reduplication, and transitions that are not properly bridged.

In this second symbolic diagram (II) I wish to suggest that really the only way to unite the parts of the system is to unite each to life. We can get only an artificial unity so long as we confine our gaze to the school system itself. We must look at it as part of the larger whole of social life. This block (A) in the center represents the school system as a whole. (1) At one side we have the home, and the two arrows represent the free interplay of influences, materials, and ideas between the home life and that of the school. (2) Below we have the relation to the natural environment, the great field of geography in the widest

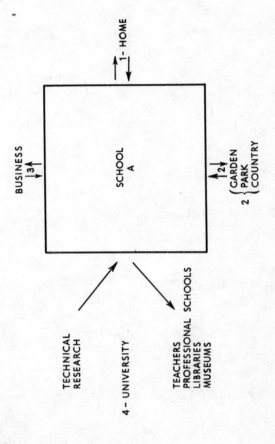

CHART II

sense. The school building has about it a natural environment. It ought to be in a garden, and the children from the garden would be led on to surrounding fields, and then into the wider country, with all its facts and forces. (3) Above is represented business life, and the necessity for free play between the school and the needs and forces of industry. (4) On the other side is the university proper, with its various phases, its laboratories, its resources in the way of libraries, museums, and professional schools.

From the standpoint of the child, the great waste in the school comes from his inability to utilize the experiences he gets outside the school in any complete and free way within the school itself; while, on the other hand, he is unable to apply in daily life what he is learning at school. That is the isolation of the school—its isolation from life. When the child gets into the schoolroom he has to put out of his mind a large part of the ideas, interests, and activities that predominate in his home and neighborhood. So the school, being unable to utilize this everyday experience, sets painfully to work, on another tack and by a variety of means, to arouse in the child an interest in school studies. While I was visiting in the city of Moline a few years ago, the superintendent told me that they found many children every year who were surprised to learn that the Mississippi river in the textbook had anything to do with the stream of water flowing past their homes. The geography being simply a matter of the schoolroom, it is more or less of an awakening to many children to find that the whole thing is nothing but a more formal and definite statement of the facts which they see, feel, and touch every day. When we think that we all live on the earth, that we live in an atmosphere, that our lives are touched at every point by the influences of the soil, flora, and fauna, by considerations of light and heat, and then think of what the school study of geography has been, we have a typical idea of the gap existing between the everyday experiences of the child and the isolated material supplied in such large measure in the school. This is but an instance, and one upon which most of us may reflect long before we take the present artificiality of the school as other than a matter of course or necessity.

Though there should be organic connection between the school and business life, it is not meant that the school is to prepare the child for any particular business, but that there should be a natural connection of the everyday life of the child with the business environment about him, and that it is the affair of the school to clarify and liberalize this connection, to bring it to consciousness, not by introducing special studies, like commercial geography and arithmetic, but by keeping alive the ordinary bonds of relation. The subject of compound-business-partnership is probably not in many of the arithmetics nowadays, though it was there not a generation ago, for the makers of textbooks said that if they left out anything they could not sell their books. This compound-business-partnership originated as far back as the sixteenth century. The joint-stock company had not been invented, and as large commerce with the Indies and Americas grew up, it was necessary to have an accumulation of capital with which to handle it. One man said, "I will put in this amount of money for six months," and another, "So much for two years," and so on. Thus by joining together they got money enough to float their commercial enterprises. Naturally, then, "compound partnership" was taught in the schools. The joint-stock company was invented; compound partnership disappeared, but the problems relating to it stayed in the arithmetics for two hundred years. They were kept after they had ceased to have practical utility, for the sake of mental discipline—they were "such hard problems, you know." A great deal of what is now in the arithmetics under the head of percentage is of the same nature. Children of twelve and thirteen years of age go through gain and loss calculations, and various forms of bank discount so complicated that the bankers long ago dispensed with them. And when it is pointed out that business is not done this way, we hear again of "mental discipline." And yet there are plenty of real connections between the experience of children and business conditions which need to be utilized and illuminated. The child should study his commercial arithmetic and geography, not as isolated things by themselves, but in their reference to his social environment. The youth needs to become acquainted with the bank as a factor in modern life, with what it does, and how it does it; and then relevant arithmetical processes would have some meaning—quite in contradistinction to the time-absorbing and mind-killing examples in percentage, partial payments, etc., found in all our arithmetics.

The connection with the university, as indicated in this chart, I need not dwell upon. I simply wish to indicate that there ought to be a free interaction between all the parts of the school system. There is much of utter triviality of subject-matter in elementary and secondary education. When we investigate it, we find that it is full of facts taught that are not facts, which have to be unlearned later on. Now, this happens because the "lower" parts of our system are not in vital connection with the "higher." The university or college, in its idea, is a place of research, where investigation is going on: a place of libraries and museums, where the best resources of the past are gathered, maintained, and organized. It is, however, as true in the school as in the university that the spirit of inquiry can be got only through and with the attitude of inquiry. The pupil must learn what has meaning, what enlarges his horizon, instead of mere trivialities. He must become acquainted with truths, instead of things that were regarded as such fifty years ago or that are taken as interesting by the misunderstanding of a partially educated teacher. It is difficult to see how these ends can be reached except as the most advanced part of the educational system is in complete interaction with the most rudimentary.

The next chart (III) is an enlargement of the second. The school building has swelled out, so to speak, the surrounding environment remaining the same, the home, the garden and country, the relation to business life and the university. The object is to show what the school must become to get out of its isolation and secure the organic connection with social life of which we have been speaking. It is not our architect's plan for the school building that we hope to have; but it is a diagrammatic representation of the idea which we want embodied in the school building. On the lower side you see the dining-room and the kitchen, at the top the wood and metal shops and the textile room for sewing and weaving. The center represents the manner in which all come together in the library; that is to say, in a collection of the intellectual resources of all kinds that throw light upon the practical work, that give it meaning and liberal value. If the four corners represent practice, the interior represents the theory of the practical activities. In other words, the object of these forms of practice in the school is not found chiefly in themselves, or in the technical skill of cooks, seamstresses, carpenters, and masons, but in their connection, on the social side, with the life without;

while on the individual side they respond to the child's need of action, of expression, of desire to do something, to be constructive and creative, instead of simply passive and conforming. Their great significance is that they keep the balance between the social and individual sides—the chart symbolizing particularly the connection with the social. Here on one side is the home. How naturally the lines of connection play back and forth between the home and the kitchen and the textile room of the school! The child can carry over what he learns in the home and utilize it in the school; and the things learned in the school he applies at home. These are the two great things in breaking down isolation, in getting connection—to have the child come to school with all the experience he has got outside the school, and to leave it with something to be immediately used in his everyday life. The child comes to the traditional school with a healthy body and a more or less unwilling mind, though, in fact, he does not bring both his body and mind with him; he has to leave his mind behind, because there is no way to use it in the school. If he had a purely abstract mind, he could bring it to school with him, but his is a concrete one, interested in concrete things, and unless these things get over into school life he cannot take his mind with him. What we want is to have the child come to school with a whole mind and a whole body, and leave school with a fuller mind and an even healthier body. And speaking of the body suggests that,

LABORATORY
RESEARCH

UNIVERSITY

LIBRARY
MUSEUM

CHART III

while there is no gymnasium in these diagrams, the active life carried on in its four corners brings with it constant physical exercise, while our gymnasium proper will deal with the particular weaknesses of children and their correction, and will attempt more consciously to build up the thoroughly sound body as the abode of the sound mind.

That the dining-room and kitchen connect with the country and its processes and products it is hardly necessary to say. Cooking may be so taught that it has no connection with country life and with the sciences that find their unity in geography. Perhaps it generally has been taught without these connections being really made. But all the materials that come into the kitchen have their origin in the country; they come from the soil, are nurtured through the influences of light and water, and represent a great variety of local environments. Through this connection, extending from the garden into the larger world, the child has his most natural introduction to the study of the sciences. Where did these things grow? What was necessary to their growth? What their relation to the soil? What the effect of different climatic conditions? and so on. We all know what the old-fashioned botany was: partly collecting flowers that were pretty, pressing and mounting them; partly pulling these flowers to pieces and giving technical names to the different parts, finding all the different leaves, naming all their different shapes and forms. It was a study of plants without any reference to the soil, to the country, or to growth. In contrast, a real study of plants takes them in their natural environment and in their uses as well, not simply as food, but in all their adaptations to the social life of man. Cooking becomes as well a most natural introduction to the study of chemistry, giving the child here also something which he can at once bring to bear upon his daily experience. I once heard a very intelligent woman say that she could not understand how science could be taught to little children, because she did not see how they could understand atoms and molecules. In other words, since she did not see how highly abstract facts could be presented to the child independently of daily experience, she could not understand how science could be taught at all. Before we smile at this remark, we need to ask ourselves if she is alone in her assumption, or whether it simply formulates the principle of almost all our school practice.

The same relations with the outside world are found in the carpentry and the textile shops. They connect with the country, as the source of their materials, with physics, as the science of applying energy, with commerce and distribution, with art in the development of architecture and decoration. They have also an intimate connection with the university on the side of its technological and engineering schools; with the laboratory and its scientific methods and results.

To go back to the square which is marked the library (Chart III, A): if you imagine rooms half in the four corners and half in the library, you will get the idea of the recitation room. That is the place where the children bring the experiences, the problems, the questions, the particular facts which they have found, and discuss them so that new light may be thrown upon them, particularly new light from the experience of others, the accumulated wisdom of the world—symbolized in the library. Here is the organic relation of theory and practice; the child not simply doing things, but getting also the *idea* of what he does; getting from the start some intellectual conception that enters into his practice and enriches it; while every idea finds, directly or indirectly, some application in experience and has some effect upon life. This, I need hardly say, fixes the position of the "book" or reading in education. Harmful as a substitute for experience, it is all-important in interpreting and expanding experience.

The remaining chart (IV) illustrates precisely the same idea. It gives the symbolic upper story of this ideal school. In the upper corners are the laboratories; in the lower corners are the studios for art work, both the graphic and auditory arts. The questions, the clinical and physical problems, arising in the kitchen and shop, are taken to the laboratories to be worked out. For instance, this past week one of the older groups of children doing practical work in weaving, which involved the use of the spinning wheel, worked out the diagrams of the direction of forces concerned in treadle and wheel, and the ratio of velocities between wheel and spindle. In the same manner, the plants with which the child has to do in cooking afford the basis for a concrete interest in botany and may be taken and studied by themselves. In a certain school in Boston science work for months was centered in the growth of the cotton plant, and yet something new was brought in every day. We hope to do similar work with all the types of plants that furnish materials for sewing and weaving. These examples will suggest, I hope, the relation which the laboratories bear to the rest of the school.

The drawing and music, or the graphic and auditory arts, represent the culmination, the idealization, the highest point of refinement of all the work carried on. I think everybody who has not a purely literary view of the subject recognizes that genuine art grows out of the work of the artisan. The art of the Renaissance was great because it grew out of the manual arts of life. It did not spring up in a separate atmosphere, however ideal, but carried on to their spiritual meaning processes found in homely and everyday forms of life. The school should observe this relationship. The merely artisan side is narrow, but the mere art, taken by itself, and grafted on from without, tends to become forced, empty, sentimental. I do not mean, of course, that all art work must be correlated in detail to the other work of the school, but

LABORATORIES
RESEARCH

UNIVERSITY

LIBRARY
MUSEUM

PHYSICAL
AND CHEMICAL
LABORATORIES

BIOLOGICAL
LABORATORY

MUSEUM

ART

MUSIC

CHART IV

simply that a spirit of union gives vitality to the art and depth and richness to the other work. All art involves physical organs— the eye and hand, the ear and voice; and yet it is something more than the mere technical skill required by the organs of expression. It involves an idea, a thought, a spiritual rendering of things; and yet it is other than any number of ideas by themselves. It is a living union of thought and the instrument of expression. This union is symbolized by saying that in the ideal school the art work might be considered to be that of the shops, passed through the alembic of library and museum into action again.

Take the textile room as an illustration of such a synthesis. I am talking about a future school, the one we hope, sometime, to have. The basal fact in that room is that it is a workshop, doing actual things in sewing, spinning, and weaving. The children come into immediate connection with the materials, with various fabrics of silk, cotton, linen, and wool. Information at once appears in connection with these materials; their origin, history, their adaptation to particular uses, and the machines of various kinds by which the raw materials are utilized. Discipline arises in dealing with the problems involved, both theoretical and practical. Whence does the culture arise? Partly from seeing all these things reflected through the medium of their scientific and historic conditions and associations, whereby the child learns to appreciate them as technical achievements, as thoughts precipitated in action; and partly because of the introduction of the art idea into the room itself. In the ideal school there would be something of this sort: first, a complete industrial museum, giving samples of materials in various stages of manufacture, and the implements, from the simplest to the most complex, used in dealing with them; then a collection of photographs and pictures illustrating the landscapes and the scenes from which the materials come, their native homes, and their places of manufacture. Such a collection would be a vivid and continual lesson in the synthesis of art, science, and industry. There would be, also, samples of the more perfect forms of textile work, as Italian, French, Japanese, and Oriental. There would be objects illustrating motives of design and decoration which have entered into production. Literature would contribute its part in its idealized representation of the world-industries, as the Penelope in the *Odyssey*—a classic in literature because the character is an adequate embodiment of a certain industrial phase of social life. So, from Homer down to the present time, there is a continuous procession of related facts which have been translated into terms of art. Music lends its share, from the Scotch song at the wheel to the spinning song of Marguerite, or of Wagner's Senta. The shop becomes a pictured museum, appealing to the eye. It would have not only materials—beautiful woods and designs—but would give a synopsis of the historical evolution of architecture in its drawings and pictures.

Thus I have attempted to indicate how the school may be connected with life so that the experience gained by the child in a familiar, commonplace way is carried over and made use of there, and what the child learns in the school is carried back and applied in everyday life, making the school an organic whole, instead of a composite of isolated parts. The isolation of studies as well as of parts of the school system disappears. Experience has its geographical aspect, its artistic and its literary, its scientific and its historical sides. All studies arise from aspects of the one earth and the one life lived upon it. We do not have a series of stratified earths, one of which is mathematical, another physical, another historical, and so on. We should not be able to live very long in any one taken by itself. We live in a world where all sides are bound together. All studies grow out of relations in the one great common world. When the child lives in varied but concrete and active relationship to this common world, his studies are naturally unified. It will no longer be a problem to correlate studies. The teacher will not have to resort to all sorts of devices to weave a little arithmetic into the history lesson, and the like. Relate the school to life, and all studies are of necessity correlated.

Moreover, if the school is related as a whole to life as a whole, its various aims and ideals—culture, discipline, information, utility—cease to be variants, for one of which we must select one study and for another another. The growth of the child in the direction of social capacity and service, his larger and more vital union with life, becomes the unifying aim; and discipline, culture, and information fall into place as phases of this growth.

I wish to add one word more about the relationship of our particular school to the University. The problem is to unify, to organize, education, to bring all its various factors together, through putting it as a whole into organic union with everyday life. That which lies back of the pedagogical school of the University is the necessity of working out something to serve as a model for such unification, extending from work beginning with the four-year-old child up through the graduate work of the University. Already we have much help from the University in scientific work planned, sometimes even in detail, by heads of the departments. The graduate student comes to us with his researches and methods, suggesting ideas and problems. The library and museum are at hand. We want to bring all things educational together; to break down the barriers that divide the education of the little child from the instruction of the maturing youth; to identify the lower and the higher education, so that it shall be demonstrated to the eye that there is no lower and higher, but simply education.

Speaking more especially with reference to the pedagogical side of the work: I suppose the oldest university chair of pedagogy in our country is about twenty years old—that of the University of Michigan, founded in the latter seventies. But there are only one or two that have tried to make a connection between theory and practice. They teach for the most part by theory, by lectures, by reference to books, rather than through the actual work of teaching itself. At Columbia, through the Teachers College, there is an extensive and close connection between the University and the training of teachers. Something has been done in one or two other places along the same line. We want an even more intimate union here, so that the University shall put all its resources at the disposition of the elementary school, contributing to the evolution of valuable subject-matter and right method, while the school in turn will be a laboratory in which the student of education sees theories and ideas demonstrated, tested, criticized, enforced, and the evolution of new truths. We want the school in its relation to the University to be a working model of a unified education.

A word as to the relation of the school to educational interests generally. I heard once that the adoption of a certain method in use in our school was objected to by a teacher on this ground: "You know that it is an experimental school. They do not work under the same conditions that we are subject to." Now, the purpose of performing an experiment is that other people need not experiment; at least need not experiment so much, may have something definite and positive to go by. An experiment demands particularly favorable conditions in order that results may be reached both freely and securely. It has to work unhampered, with all the needed resources at command. Laboratories lie back of all the great business enterprises of today, back of every great factory, every railway and steamship system. Yet the laboratory is not a business enterprise; it does not aim to secure for itself the conditions of business life, nor does the commercial undertaking repeat the laboratory. There is a difference between working out and testing a new truth, or a new method, and applying it on a wide scale, making it available for the mass of men, making it commercial. But the first thing is to discover the truth, to afford all necessary facilities, for this is the most practical thing in the world in the long run. We do not expect to have other schools literally imitate what we do. A working model is not something to be copied; it is to afford a demonstration of the feasibility of the principle, and of the methods which make it feasible. So (to come back to our own point) we want here to work out the problem of the unity, the organization of the school system in itself, and to do this by relating it so intimately to life as to demonstrate the possibility and necessity of such organization for all education.

IV
The Psychology of Elementary Education

Naturally, most of the public is interested in what goes on day by day in a school in direct relation to the children there. This is true of parents who send their boys and girls for the sake of the personal results they wish to secure, not for the sake of contributing to educational theory. In the main, it is true of visitors to a school who recognize, in varying degrees, what is actually done with the children before their eyes, but who rarely have either the interest or the time to consider the work in relation to underlying problems. A school cannot lose sight of this aspect of its work, since only by attending to it can the school retain the confidence of its patrons and the presence of its pupils.

Nevertheless a school conducted by a department of a university must have another aspect. From the university standpoint, the most important part of its work is the scientific—the contribution it makes to the progress of educational thinking. The aim of educating a certain number of children would hardly justify a university in departing from the tradition which limits it to those who have completed their secondary instruction. Only the scientific aim, the conduct of a laboratory, comparable to other scientific laboratories, can furnish a reason for the maintenance by a university of an elementary school. Such a school is a laboratory of applied psychology. That is, it has a place for the study of mind as manifested and developed in the child, and for the search after materials and agencies that seem most likely to fulfil and further the conditions of normal growth.

It is not a normal school or a department for the training of teachers. It is not a model school. It is not intended to demonstrate any one special idea or doctrine. Its task is the problem of viewing the education of the child in the light of the principles of mental activity and processes of growth made known by modern psychology. The problem by its nature is an infinite one. All that any school can do is to make contributions here and there, and to stand for the necessity of considering education, both theoretically and practically, in this light. This being the end, the school conditions must, of course, agree. To endeavor to study the process and laws of growth under such artificial conditions as prevent many of the chief facts of child life from showing themselves is an obvious absurdity.

In its practical aspect, this laboratory problem takes the form of the construction of a course of study which harmonizes with the natural history of the growth of the child in capacity and experience. The question is the selection of the kind, variety, and due proportion of subjects, answering most definitely to the dominant needs and powers of a given period of growth, and of those modes of presentation that will cause the selected material to enter vitally into growth. We cannot admit too fully or too freely the limits of our knowledge and the depths of our ignorance in these matters. No one has a complete hold scientifically upon the chief psychological facts of any one year of child life. It would be sheer presumption to claim that just the material best fitted to promote this growth has as yet been discovered. The assumption of an educational laboratory is rather that enough is known of the conditions and modes of growth to make intelligent inquiry possible; and that it is only by acting upon what is already known

that more can be found out. The chief point is such experimentation as will add to our reasonable convictions. The demand is to
secure arrangements that will permit and encourage freedom of
investigation; that will give some assurance that important facts
will not be forced out of sight; conditions that will enable the
educational practice indicated by the inquiry to be sincerely
acted upon, without the distortion and suppression arising from
undue dependence upon tradition and preconceived notions. It is
in this sense that the school would be an experimental station in
education.

What, then, are the chief working hypotheses that have been
adopted from psychology? What educational counterparts have
been hit upon as in some degree in line with the adopted
psychology?

The discussion of these questions may be approached by pointing out a contrast between contemporary psychology and the psychology of former days. The contrast is a triple one. Earlier psychology regarded mind as a purely individual affair in direct and
naked contact with an external world. The only question asked
was of the ways in which the world and the mind acted upon each
other. The entire process recognized would have been in theory
exactly the same if there were one mind living alone in the universe. At present the tendency is to conceive individual mind as a
function of social life—as not capable of operating or developing

by itself, but as requiring continual stimulus from social agencies, and finding its nutrition in social supplies. The idea of heredity has made familiar the notion that the equipment of the individual, mental as well as physical, is an inheritance from the race: a capital inherited by the individual from the past and held in trust by him for the future. The idea of evolution has made familiar the notion that mind cannot be regarded as an individual, monopolistic possession, but represents the outworkings of the endeavor and thought of humanity; that it is developed in an environment which is social as well as physical, and that social needs and aims have been most potent in shaping it—and the chief difference between savagery and civilization is not in the naked nature which each faces, but the social heredity and social medium.

Studies of childhood have made it equally apparent that this socially acquired inheritance operates in the individual only under present social stimuli. Nature must indeed furnish its physical stimuli of light, sound, heat, etc., but the significance attaching to these, the interpretation made of them, depends upon the ways in which the society in which the child lives acts and reacts in reference to them. The bare physical stimulus of light is not the entire reality; the interpretation given to it through social activities and thinking confers upon it its wealth of meaning. It is through imitation, suggestion, direct instruction, and even more indirect unconscious tuition, that the child learns to estimate and treat the bare physical stimuli. It is through the social agencies that he recapitulates in a few short years the progress which it has taken the race slow centuries to work out.

Educational practice has exhibited an unconscious adaptation to and harmony with the prevailing psychology; both grew out of the same soil. Just as mind was supposed to get its filling by direct contact with the world, so all the needs of instruction were thought to be met by bringing the child mind into direct relation with various bodies of external fact labeled geography, arithmetic, grammar, etc. That these classified sets of facts were simply selections from the social life of the past was overlooked; equally so that they had been generated out of social situations and represented the answers found for social needs. No social element was found in the subject-matter nor in the intrinsic appeal which it made to the child; it was located wholly outside in the teacher— in the encouragements, admonitions, urgings, and devices of the instructor in getting the child's mind to work upon a material which in itself was only accidentally lighted up by any social gleam. It was forgotten that the maximum appeal, and the full meaning in the life of the child, could be secured only when the studies were presented, not as bare external studies, but from the standpoint of the relation they bear to the life of society. It was forgotten that to become integral parts of the child's conduct and character they must be assimilated, not as mere items of information, but as organic parts of his present needs and aims—which in turn are social.

In the second place, the older psychology was a psychology of knowledge, of intellect. Emotion and endeavor occupied but an incidental and derivative place. Much was said about sensations—next to nothing about movements. There was discussion of ideas and of whether they originated in sensations or in some innate mental faculty; but the possibility of their origin in and from the needs of action was ignored. Their influence upon conduct, upon behavior, was regarded as an external attachment. Now we believe (to use the words of Mr. William James) that the intellect, the sphere of sensations and ideas, is but a "middle department which we sometimes take to be final, failing to see, amidst the monstrous diversity of the length and complications of the cogitations which may fill it, that it can have but one essential function—the function of defining the direction which our activity, immediate or remote, shall take."

Here also was a pre-established harmony between educational practice and psychological theory. Knowledge in the schools was isolated and made an end in itself. Facts, laws, information have been the staple of the curriculum. The controversy in educational theory and practice was between those who relied more upon the sense element in knowledge, upon contact with things, upon object-lessons, etc., and those who emphasized abstract ideas, generalizations, etc.—reason, so called, but in reality other people's ideas as formulated in books. In neither case was there any attempt to connect either the sense training or the logical operations with the problems and interests of the life of practice. Here again an educational transformation is indicated if we are to suppose that our psychological theories stand for any truths of life.

The third point of contrast lies in the modern conception of the mind as essentially a process—a process of growth, not a fixed thing. According to the older view mind was mind, and that was the whole story. Mind was the same throughout, because fitted out with the same assortment of faculties whether in child or adult. If any difference was made it was simply that some of these ready-made faculties—such as memory—came into play at an earlier time, while others, such as judging and inferring, made their appearance only after the child, through memorizing drills, had been reduced to complete dependence upon the thought of others. The only important difference that was recognized was one of quantity, of amount. The boy was a little man and his mind was a little mind—in everything but the size the same as that of the adult, having its own ready-furnished equipment of faculties of attention, memory, etc. Now we believe in the mind as a growing affair, and hence as essentially changing, presenting distinctive phases of capacity and interest at different periods. These are all one and the same in the sense of continuity of life, but all different, in that each has its own distinctive claims and offices. "First the blade, then the ear, and then the full corn in the ear."

It is hardly possible to overstate the agreement of education and psychology at this point. The course of study was thoroughly, even if unconsciously, controlled by the assumption that since mind and its faculties are the same throughout, the subject-matter of the adult, logically arranged facts and principles, is the natural "study" of the child—simplified and made easier of course, since the wind must be tempered to the shorn lamb. The outcome was the traditional course of study in which again child and adult minds are absolutely identified, except as regards the mere matter of amount or quantity of power. The entire range of the universe is first subdivided into sections called studies; then each one of these studies is broken up into bits, and some one bit assigned to a certain year of the course. No order of development was recognized—it was enough that the earlier parts were made easier than the later. To use the pertinent illustration of Mr. W. S. Jackman in stating the absurdity of this sort of curriculum: "It must seem to geography teachers that Heaven smiled on them when it ordained but four or five continents, because starting in far enough along the course it was so easy, that it really seemed to be natural, to give one continent to each grade, and then come out right in the eight years."

If once more we are in earnest with the idea of mind as growth, this growth carrying with it typical features distinctive of its various stages, it is clear that an educational transformation is again indicated. It is clear that the selection and grading of material in the course of study must be done with reference to proper nutrition of the dominant directions of activity in a given period, not with reference to chopped-up sections of a ready-made universe of knowledge.

It is, of course, comparatively easy to lay down general propositions like the foregoing; easy to use them to criticize existing school conditions; easy by means of them to urge the necessity of something different. But art is long. The difficulty is in carrying such conceptions into effect—in seeing just what materials and methods, in what proportion and arrangement, are available and helpful at a given time. Here again we must fall back upon the idea of the laboratory. There is no answer in advance to such questions as these. Tradition does not give it because tradition is founded upon a radically different psychology. Mere reasoning cannot give it because it is a question of fact. It is only by trying that such things can be found out. To refuse to try, to stick blindly to tradition, because the search for the truth involves experimentation in the region of the unknown, is to refuse the only step which can introduce rational conviction into education.

Hence the following statement simply reports various lines of inquiry started during the last five years, with some of the results more recently indicated. These results can, of course, make no claim to be other than tentative, excepting in so far as a more definite consciousness of what the problems are, clearing the way for more intelligent action in the future, is a definitive advance. It should also be stated that practically it has not as yet been possible, in many cases, to act adequately upon the best ideas obtained, because of administrative difficulties, due to lack of funds —difficulties centering in the lack of a proper building and appliances, and in inability to pay the amounts necessary to secure the complete time of teachers in some important lines. Indeed, with the growth of the school in numbers, and in the age and maturity of pupils, it is becoming a grave question how long it is fair to the experiment to carry it on without more adequate facilities.

In coming now to speak of the educational answers which have been sought for the psychological hypotheses, it is convenient to start from the matter of the stages of growth. The first stage (found in the child, say, of from four to eight years of age) is characterized by directness of social and personal interests, and by directness and promptness of relationship between impressions, ideas, and action. The demand for a motor outlet for expression is urgent and immediate. Hence the subject-matter for these years is selected from phases of life entering into the child's own social surroundings, and, as far as may be, capable of reproduction by him in something approaching social form—in play, games, occupations, or miniature industrial arts, stories, pictorial imagination, and conversation. At first the material is such as lies nearest the child himself, the family life and its neighborhood setting; it then goes on to something slightly more remote, social occupations (especially those having to do with the interdependence of city and country life), and then extends itself to the historical evolution of typical occupations and of the social forms connected with them. The material is not presented as lessons, as something to be learned, but rather as something to be taken up into the child's own experience, through his own activities, in weaving, cooking, shopwork, modeling, dramatic plays, conversation, discussion, story-telling, etc. These in turn are direct agencies. They are forms of motor or expressive activity. They are emphasized so as to dominate the school program, in order that the intimate connection between knowing and doing, so characteristic of this period of child life, may be maintained. The aim, then, is not for the child to go to school as a place apart, but rather in the school so to recapitulate typical phases of his experience outside of school, as to enlarge, enrich, and gradually formulate it.

In the second period, extending from eight or nine to eleven or twelve, the aim is to recognize and respond to the change which comes into the child from his growing sense of the possibility of more permanent and objective results and of the necessity for the control of agencies for the skill necessary to reach these results. When the child recognizes distinct and enduring ends which stand out and demand attention on their own account, the previous vague and fluid unity of life is broken up. The mere play of activity no longer directly satisfies. It must be felt to accomplish something—to lead up to a definite and abiding outcome. Hence the recognition of rules of action—that is, of regular means appropriate to reaching permanent results—and of the value of mastering special processes so as to give skill in their use.

Hence, on the educational side, the problem is, as regards the subject-matter, to differentiate the vague unity of experience into characteristic typical phases, selecting such as clearly illustrate the importance to mankind of command over specific agencies and methods of thought and action in realizing its highest aims. The problem on the side of method is an analogous one: to bring the child to recognize the necessity of a similar development within himself—the need of securing for himself practical and intellectual control of such methods of work and inquiry as will enable him to realize results for himself.

On the more direct social side, American history (especially that of the period of colonization) is selected as furnishing a typical example of patience, courage, ingenuity, and continual judgment in adapting means to ends, even in the face of great hazard and obstacle; while the material itself is so definite, vivid, and human as to come directly within the range of the child's representative and constructive imagination and thus becomes, vicariously at least, a part of his own expanding consciousness. Since the aim is not "covering the ground," but knowledge of social processes used to secure social results, no attempt is made to go over the entire history, in chronological order, of America. Rather a series of types is taken up: Chicago and the northwestern Mississippi valley; Virginia, New York, and the Puritans and Pilgrims in New England. The aim is to present a variety of climatic and local conditions, to show the different sorts of obstacles and helps that people found, and a variety of historic traditions and customs and purposes of different people.

The method involves presentation of a large amount of detail, of minutiae of surroundings, tools, clothing, household utensils, foods, modes of living day by day, so that the child can reproduce the material as life, not as mere historic information. In this way, social processes and results become realities. Moreover, to the personal and dramatic identification of the child with the social life studied, characteristic of the earlier period, there now supervenes an *intellectual* identification—the child puts himself at the standpoint of the problems that have to be met and rediscovers, so far as may be, ways of meeting them.

The general standpoint—the adaptation of means to ends—

controls also the work in science. For purposes of convenience, this may be regarded as now differentiated into two sides—the geographical and the experimental. Since, as just stated, the history work depends upon an appreciation of the natural environment as affording resources and presenting urgent problems, considerable attention is paid to the physiography, mountains, rivers, plains, and lines of natural travel and exchange, flora and fauna of each of the colonies. This is connected with field excursions in order that the child may be able to supply from observation, as far as possible, the data to be used by constructive imagination, in reproducing more remote environments.

The experimental side devotes itself to a study of processes which yield typical results of value to men. The activity of the child in the earlier period is directly productive, rather than investigative. His experiments are modes of active doing—almost as much so as his play and games. Later he tries to find out how various materials or agencies are manipulated in order to give certain results. It is thus clearly distinguished from experimentation in the scientific sense—such as is appropriate to the secondary period—where the aim is the discovery of facts and verification of principles. Since the practical interest predominates, it is a study of applied science rather than of pure science. For instance, processes are selected found to have been of importance in colonial life—bleaching, dyeing, soap and candle-making, manufacture of pewter dishes, making of cider and vinegar, leading to some study of chemical agencies, of oils, fats, elementary metallurgy. "Physics" is commenced from the same applied standpoint. A study is made of the use and transfer of energy in the spinning-wheel and looms; everyday uses of mechanical principles are taken up—in locks, scales, etc., going on later to electric appliances and devices—bells, the telegraph, etc.

The relation of means to ends is emphasized also in other lines of work. In art attention is given to practical questions of perspective, of proportion of spaces and masses, balance, effect of color combinations and contrasts, etc. In cooking, the principles of food-composition and of effects of various agencies upon these elements are taken up, so that the children may deduce, as far as possible, their own rules. In sewing, methods of cutting, fitting (as applied to dolls' clothing) come up, and later on the technical sequence of stitches, etc.

It is clear that with the increasing differentiation of lines of work and interest, leading to greater individuality and independence in various studies, great care must be taken to find the balance between, on one side, undue separation and isolation, and, on the other, a miscellaneous and casual attention to a large number of topics, without adequate emphasis and distinctiveness to any. The first principle makes work mechanical and formal, divorces it from the life-experience of the child and from effective influence upon conduct. The second makes it scrappy and vague and leaves the child without definite command of his own powers or clear consciousness of purposes. It is perhaps only in the present year that the specific principle of the conscious relation of means to ends has emerged as the unifying principle of this period; and it is hoped that emphasis of this in all lines of work will have a decidedly cumulative and unifying effect upon the child's development.

Nothing has been said, as yet, of one of the most important agencies or means in extending and controlling experience—command of the social or conventional symbols—symbols of language, including those of quantity. The importance of these instrumentalities is so great that the traditional or three R's curriculum is based upon them—from 60 to 80 per cent of the time program of the first four or five years of elementary schools being devoted to them, the smaller figure representing selected rather than average schools.

These subjects are social in a double sense. They represent the tools which society has evolved in the past as the instruments of its intellectual pursuits. They represent the keys which will unlock to the child the wealth of social capital which lies beyond the possible range of his limited individual experience. While these two points of view must always give these arts a highly important place in education, they also make it necessary that certain conditions should be observed in their introduction and use. In a wholesale and direct application of the studies no account is taken of these conditions. The chief problem at present relating to the three R's is recognition of these conditions and the adaptation of work to them.

The conditions may be reduced to two: (1) The need that the child shall have in his own personal and vital experience a varied background of contact and acquaintance with realities, social and physical. This is necessary to prevent symbols from becoming a purely second-hand and conventional substitute for reality. (2) The need that the more ordinary, direct, and personal experience of the child shall furnish problems, motives, and interests that necessitate recourse to books for their solution, satisfaction, and pursuit. Otherwise, the child approaches the book without intellectual hunger, without alertness, without a questioning attitude, and the result is the one so deplorably common: such abject dependence upon books as weakens and cripples vigor of thought and inquiry, combined with reading for mere random stimulation of fancy, emotional indulgence, and flight from the world of reality into a make-believe land.

The problem here is then (1) to furnish the child with a sufficiently large amount of personal activity in occupations, expression, conversation, construction, and experimentation, so that his individuality, moral and intellectual, shall not be swamped by a disproportionate amount of the experience of others to which books introduce him; and (2) so to conduct this more direct experience as to make the child feel the need of resort to and command of the traditional social tools—furnish him with motives and make his recourse to them intelligent, an addition to his powers, instead of a servile dependency. When this problem shall be solved, work in language, literature, and number will not be a combination of mechanical drill, formal analysis, and appeal, even if unconscious, to sensational interests; and there will not be the slightest reason to fear that books and all that relates to them will not take the important place to which they are entitled.

It is hardly necessary to say that the problem is not yet solved. The common complaints that children's progress in these traditional school studies is sacrificed to the newer subjects that have come into the curiculum is sufficient evidence that the exact balance is not yet struck. The experience thus far in the school, even if not demonstrative, indicates the following probable results: (1) the more direct modes of activity, constructive and occupation work, scientific observation, experimentation, etc., present plenty of opportunities and occasions for the necessary use of reading, writing (and spelling), and number work. These things may be introduced, then, not as isolated studies, but as organic outgrowths of the child's experience. The problem is, in a systematic and progressive way, to take advantage of these occasions.

(2) The additional vitality and meaning which these studies thus secure make possible a very considerable reduction of the time ordinarily devoted to them. (3) The final use of the symbols, whether in reading, calculation, or composition, is more intelligent, less mechanical; more active, less passively receptive; more an increase of power, less a mere mode of enjoyment.

On the other hand, increasing experience seems to make clear the following points: (1) that it is possible, in the early years, to appeal, in teaching the recognition and use of symbols, to the child's power of production and creation; as much so in principle as in other lines of work seemingly much more direct, and that there is the advantage of a limited and definite result by which the child may measure his progress. (2) Failure sufficiently to take account of this fact resulted in an undue postponement of some phases of these lines of work, with the effect that the child, having progressed to a more advanced plane intellectually, feels what earlier might have been a form of power and creation to be an irksome task. (3) There is a demand for periodic concentration and alternation in the school program of the time devoted to these studies—and of all studies where mastery of technique or special method is advisable. That is to say, instead of carrying all subjects simultaneously and at an equal pace upon the program, at times one must be brought to the foreground and others relegated to the background, until the child is brought to the point of recognizing that he has a power or skill which he can now go ahead and use independently.

The third period of elementary education is upon the borderland of secondary. It comes when the child has a sufficient acquaintance of a fairly direct sort with various forms of reality and modes of activity; and when he has sufficiently mastered the methods, the tools of thought, inquiry, and activity, appropriate to various phases of experience, to be able profitably to specialize upon distinctive studies and arts for technical and intellectual aims. While the school has a number of children who are in this period, the school has not, of course, been in existence long enough so that any typical inferences can be safely drawn. There certainly seems to be reason to hope, however, that with the consciousness of difficulties, needs, and resources gained in the experience of the last five years, children can be brought to and through this period without sacrifice of thoroughness, mental discipline, or command of technical tools of learning, and with a positive enlargement of life, and a wider, freer, and more open outlook upon it.

V
Froebel's Educational Principles

One of the traditions of the Elementary School of the University of Chicago is of a visitor who, in its early days, called to see the kindergarten. On being told that the school had not as yet established one, she asked if there were not singing, drawing, manual training, plays and dramatizations, and attention to the children's social relations. When her questions were answered in the affirmative, she remarked, both triumphantly and indignantly, that that was what she understood by a kindergarten, and that she did not know what was meant by saying that the school had no kindergarten. The remark was perhaps justified in spirit, if not in letter. At all events, it suggests that in a certain sense the school endeavors throughout its whole course—now including children between four and thirteen—to carry into effect certain principles which Froebel was perhaps the first consciously to set forth. Speaking still in general, these principles are:

1. That the primary business of school is to train children in co-operative and mutually helpful living; to foster in them the consciousness of mutual interdependence; and to help them practically in making the adjustments that will carry this spirit into overt deeds.

2. That the primary root of all educative activity is in the instinctive, impulsive attitudes and activities of the child, and not in the presentation and application of external material, whether through the ideas of others or through the senses; and that, accordingly, numberless spontaneous activities of children, plays, games, mimic efforts, even the apparently meaningless motions of infants—exhibitions previously ignored as trivial, futile, or even condemned as positively evil—are capable of educational use; nay, are the foundation-stones of educational method.

3. That these individual tendencies and activities are organ-

117

ized and directed through the uses made of them in keeping up the co-operative living already spoken of; taking advantage of them to reproduce on the child's plane the typical doings and occupations of the larger, maturer society into which he is finally to go forth; and that it is through production and creative use that valuable knowledge is secured and clinched.

So far as these statements correctly represent Froebel's educational philosophy, the School should be regarded as its exponent. An attempt is being made to act upon them with as much faith and sincerity in their application to children of twelve as to children of four. This attempt, however, to assume what might be called the kindergarten attitude throughout the whole school makes necessary certain modifications of the work done in what is more technically known as the kindergarten period—that is, with the children between the ages of four and six. It is necessary only to state reasons for believing that in spite of the apparently radical character of some of them they are true to the spirit of Froebel.

AS REGARDS PLAY AND GAMES

Play is not to be identified with anything which the child externally does. It rather designates his mental attitude in its entirety and in its unity. It is the free play, the interplay, of all the child's powers, thoughts, and physical movements, in embodying, in a satisfying form, his own images and interests. Negatively, it is freedom from economic pressure—the necessities of getting a living and supporting others—and from the fixed responsibilities attaching to the special callings of the adult. Positively, it means that the supreme end of the child is fulness of growth—fulness of realization of his budding powers, a realization which continually carries him on from one plane to another.

This is a very general statement and, taken in its generality, is so vague as to be innocent of practical bearing. Its significance in detail, in application, however, means the possibility, and in many respects the necessity, of quite a radical change of kindergarten procedure. To state it baldly, the fact that "play" denotes the psychological attitude of the child, not his outward performances, means complete emancipation from the necessity of following any given or prescribed system, or sequence of gifts, plays, or occupations. The judicious teacher will certainly look for suggestions to the activities mentioned by Froebel (in his *Mother-Play* and elsewhere), and to those set forth in such minute detail by his disciples; but she will also remember that the principle of play requires her carefully to investigate and criticize these things, and decide whether they are really activities for her own children, or just things which may have been vital in the past to children living in different social conditions. So far as occupations, games, etc., simply perpetuate those of Froebel and his earlier disciples, it may fairly be said that in many respects the presumption is against them—the presumption is that in the worship of the external doings discussed by Froebel we have ceased to be loyal to his principle.

The teacher must be absolutely free to get suggestions from any and from every source, asking herself but these two questions: Will the proposed mode of play appeal to the child as his own? Is it something of which he has the instinctive roots in himself, and which will mature the capacities that are struggling for manifestation in him? And again: Will the proposed activity give that sort of expression to these impulses that will carry the child on to a higher plane of consciousness and action, instead of merely exciting him and then leaving him just where he was before, plus a certain amount of nervous exhaustion and appetite for more excitation in the future?

There is every evidence that Froebel studied carefully—inductively we might now say—the children's plays of his own time, and the games which mothers played with their infants. He also took great pains—as in his *Mother-Play*—to point out that certain principles of large import were involved. He had to bring his generation to consciousness of the fact that these things were not merely trivial and childish because done by children, but were essential factors in their growth. But I do not see the slightest evidence that he supposed that just these plays, and only these plays, had meaning, or that his philosophic explanation had any motive beyond that just suggested. On the contrary, I believe that he expected his followers to exhibit their following by continuing his own study of contemporary conditions and activities, rather than by literally adhering to the plays he had collected. Moreover, it is hardly likely that Froebel himself would contend that in his interpretation of these games he did more than take advantage of the best psychological and philosophical insight available to him at the time; and we may suppose that he would have been the first to welcome the growth of a better and more extensive psychology (whether general, experimental, or as child study), and would avail himself of its results to reinterpret the activities, to discuss them more critically, going from the new standpoint into the reasons that make them educationally valuable.

SYMBOLISM

It must be remembered that much of Froebel's symbolism is the product of two peculiar conditions of his own life and work. In the first place, on account of inadequate knowledge at that time of the physiological and psychological facts and principles of child growth, he was often forced to resort to strained and artificial explanations of the value attaching to the plays, etc. To the impartial observer it is obvious that many of his statements are cumbrous and far-fetched, giving abstract philosophical reasons

121

for matters that may now receive a simple, everyday formulation. In the second place, the general political and social conditions of Germany were such that it was impossible to conceive continuity between the free, co-operative social life of the kindergarten and that of the world outside. Accordingly, he could not regard the "occupations" of the schoolroom as literal reproductions of the ethical principles involved in community life—the latter were often too restricted and authoritative to serve as worthy models.

Accordingly he was compelled to think of them as symbolic of abstract ethical and philosophical principles. There certainly is change enough and progress enough in the social conditions of the United States of today, as compared with those of the Germany of his day, to justify making kindergarten activities more natural, more direct, and more real representations of current life than Froebel's disciples have done. Even as it is, the disparity of Froebel's philosophy with German political ideals has made the authorities in Germany suspicious of the kindergarten, and has been undoubtedly one force operating in transforming its social simplicity into an involved intellectual technique.

IMAGINATION AND PLAY

An excessive emphasis on symbolism is sure to influence the treatment of imagination. It is of course true that a little child lives in a world of imagination. In one sense, he can only "make believe." His activities represent or stand for the life that he sees going on around him. Because they are thus representative they may be termed symbolic, but it should be remembered that this make-believe or symbolism has reference to the activities suggested. Unless they are, to the child, as real and definite as the adult's activities are to him, the inevitable result is artificiality, nervous strain, and either physical and emotional excitement or else deadening of powers.

There has been a curious, almost unaccountable, tendency in the kindergarten to assume that because the value of the activity lies in what it stands for to the child, therefore the materials used must be as artificial as possible, and that one must keep carefully away from real things and real acts on the part of the child. Thus one hears of gardening activities which are carried on by sprinkling grains of sand for seeds; the child sweeps and dusts a make-believe room with make-believe brooms and cloths; he sets a table using only paper cut in the flat (and even then cut with reference to geometric design, rather than to dishes), instead of toy tea things with which the child outside of the kindergarten plays. Dolls, toy locomotives, and trains of cars, etc., are tabooed as altogether too grossly real—and hence not cultivating the child's imagination.

All this is surely mere superstition. The imaginative play of the child's mind comes through the cluster of suggestions, reminiscences, and anticipations that gather about the things he uses. The more natural and straightforward these are, the more definite basis there is for calling up and holding together all the allied suggestions which make his imaginative play really representative. The simple cooking, dishwashing, dusting, etc., which children do are no more prosaic or utilitarian to them than would be, say, the game of the Five Knights. To the children these occupations are surcharged with a sense of the mysterious values that attach to whatever their elders are concerned with. The materials, then, must be as "real," as direct and straightforward, as opportunity permits.

But the principle does not end here—the reality symbolized must also lie within the capacities of the child's own appreciation. It is sometimes thought the use of the imagination is profitable in the degree it stands for very remote metaphysical and spiritual principles. In the great majority of such cases it is safe to say that the adult deceives himself. He is conscious of both the reality and the symbol, and hence of the relation between them. But since the truth or reality represented is far beyond the reach of the child, the supposed symbol is not a symbol to him at all. It is simply a positive thing on its own account. Practically about all he gets out of it is its own physical and sensational meaning, plus, very often, a glib facility in phrases and attitudes that he learns are expected of him by the teacher—without, however, any mental counterpart. We often teach insincerity, and instil sentimentalism, and foster sensationalism when we think we are teaching spiritual truths by means of symbols. The realities reproduced, therefore, by the child should be of as familiar, direct, and real a character as possible. It is largely for this reason that in the kindergarten of our School the work centers so much about the reproduction of home and neighborhood life. This brings us to the topic of subject-matter.

SUBJECT-MATTER

The home life in its setting of house, furniture, utensils, etc., together with the occupations carried on in the home, offers, accordingly, material which is in a direct and real relationship to the child, and which he naturally tends to reproduce in imaginative form. It is also sufficiently full of ethical relations and suggestive of moral duties to afford plenty of food for the child on his moral side. The program is comparatively unambitious compared with that of many kindergartens, but it may be questioned whether there are not certain positive advantages in this limitation of the subject-matter. When much ground is covered (the work going over, say, industrial society, army, church, state, etc.), there is a tendency for the work to become oversymbolic. So much of this material lies beyond the experience and capacities of the child of four and five that practically all he gets out of it is the physical and emotional reflex—he does not get any real penetration into the material itself. Moreover, there is danger, in these ambitious programs, of an unfavorable reaction upon the child's own intellectual attitude. Having covered pretty much the whole universe in a purely make-believe fashion, he becomes blasé, loses his natural hunger for the simple things of direct experience, and approaches the material of the first grades of the primary school with a feeling that he has had all that already. The later years of a child's life have their own rights, and a superficial, merely emotional anticipation is likely to do the child serious injury.

Moreover, there is danger that a mental habit of jumping rapidly from one topic to another be induced. The little child has a good deal of patience and endurance of a certain type. It is true that he has a liking for novelty and variety; that he soon wearies of an activity that does not lead out into new fields and open up new paths for exploration. My plea, however, is not for monotony. There is sufficient variety in the activities, furnishings, and instrumentalities of the homes from which the children come to give continual diversity. It touches the civic and the industrial life at this and that point; these concerns can be brought in, when desirable, without going beyond the unity of the main topic. Thus there is an opportunity to foster that sense which is at the basis of attention and of all intellectual growth—a sense of continuity.

This continuity is often interfered with by the very methods that aim at securing it. From the child's standpoint unity lies in the subject-matter—in the present case, in the fact that he is always dealing with one thing: home life. Emphasis is continually passing from one phase of this life to another; one occupation after another, one piece of furniture after another, one relation after another, etc., receive attention; but they all fall into building up one and the same mode of living, although bringing now this feature, now that, into prominence. The child is working all the time *within a unity*, giving different phases of its clearness and definiteness, and bringing them into coherent connection with each other. When there is a great diversity of subject-matter, continuity is apt to be sought simply on the formal side; that is, in schemes of sequence, "schools of work," a rigid program of development followed with every topic, a "thought for the day" from which the work is not supposed to stray. As a rule such sequence is purely intellectual, hence is grasped only by the teacher, quite passing over the head of the child. Hence the program for the year, term, month, week, etc., should be made out on the basis of estimating how much of the common subject-matter can be covered in that time, not on the basis of intellectual or ethical principles. This will give both definiteness and elasticity.

METHOD

The peculiar problem of the early grades is, of course, to get hold of the child's natural impulses and instincts, and to utilize them so that the child is carried on to a higher plane of perception and judgment, and equipped with more efficient habits; so

127

that he has an enlarged and deepened consciousness and increased control of powers of action. Wherever this result is not reached, play results in mere amusement and not in educative growth.

Upon the whole, constructive or "built up" work (with, of course, the proper alternation of story, song, and game which may be connected, so far as is desirable, with the ideas involved in the construction) seems better fitted than anything else to secure these two factors—initiation in the child's own impulse and termination upon a higher plane. It brings the child in contact with a great variety of material: wood, tin, leather, yarn, etc.; it supplies a motive for using these materials in real ways instead of going through exercises having no meaning except a remote symbolic one; it calls into play alertness of the senses and acuteness of observation; it demands clear-cut imagery of the ends to be accomplished, and requires ingenuity and invention in planning; it makes necessary concentrated attention and personal responsibility in execution, while the results are in such tangible form that the child may be led to judge his own work and improve his standards.

A word should be said regarding the psychology of imitation and suggestion in relation to kindergarten work. There is no doubt that the little child is highly imitative and open to suggestions; there is no doubt that his crude powers and immature consciousness need to be continually enriched and directed through these channels. But on this account it is imperative to discriminate between a use of imitation and suggestion which is so external as to be thoroughly non-psychological, and a use which is justified through its organic relation to the child's own activities. As a general principle no activity should be *originated* by imitation. The start must come from the child; the model or copy may then be supplied in order to assist the child in imaging more definitely what it is that he really wants—in bringing him to consciousness. Its value is not as model to copy in action, but as guide to clearness and adequacy of conception. Unless the child can get away from it to his own imagery when it comes to execution, he is rendered servile and dependent, not developed. Imitation comes in to reinforce and help out, not to initiate.

There is no ground for holding that the teacher should not suggest anything to the child until he has *consciously* expressed a want in that direction. A sympathetic teacher is quite likely to know more clearly than the child himself what his own instincts are and mean. But the suggestion must *fit in* with the dominant mode of growth in the child; it must serve simply as stimulus to bring forth more adequately what the child is already blindly striving to do. Only by watching the child and seeing the attitude that he assumes toward suggestions can we tell whether they are operating as factors in furthering the child's growth, or whether

129

they are external, arbitrary impositions interfering with normal growth.

The same principle applies even more strongly to so-called dictation work. Nothing is more absurd than to suppose that there is no middle term between leaving a child to his own unguided fancies and likes or controlling his activities by a formal succession of dictated directions. As just intimated, it is the teacher's business to know what powers are striving for utterance at a given period in the child's development, and what sorts of activity will bring these to helpful expression, in order then to supply the requisite stimuli and needed materials. The suggestion, for instance, of a playhouse, the suggestion that comes from seeing objects that have already been made to furnish it, from seeing other children at work, is quite sufficient definitely to direct the activities of a normal child of five. Imitation and suggestion come in naturally and inevitably, but only as instruments to help him carry out his own wishes and ideas. They serve to make him realize, to bring to consciousness, what he already is striving for in a vague, confused, and therefore ineffective way. From the psychological standpoint it may safely be said that when a teacher has to rely upon a series of dictated directions, it is just because the child has no image of his own of what is to be done or why it is to be done. Instead, therefore, of gaining power of control by conforming to directions, he is really losing it—made dependent upon an external source.

In conclusion, it may be pointed out that such subject-matter and the method connect directly with the work of the six-year-old children (corresponding to the first grade of primary work). The play reproduction of the home life passes naturally on into a more extended and serious study of the larger social occupations upon which the home is dependent; while the continually increasing demands made upon the child's own ability to plan and execute carry him over into more controlled use of attention upon more distinctively intellectual topics. It must not be forgotten that the readjustment needed to secure continuity between "kindergarten" and "first-grade" work cannot be brought about wholly from the side of the latter. The school change must be as gradual and insensible as that in the growth of the child. This is impossible unless the subprimary work surrenders whatever isolates it, and hospitably welcomes whatever materials and resources will keep pace with the full development of the child's powers, and thus keep him always prepared, ready, for the next work he has to do.

VI
The Psychology of Occupations

By occupation is not meant any kind of "busy work" or exercises that may be given to a child in order to keep him out of mischief or idleness when seated at his desk. By occupation I mean a mode of activity on the part of the child which reproduces, or runs parallel to, some form of work carried on in social life. In the University Elementary School these occupations are represented by the shopwork with wood and tools; by cooking, sewing, and by the textile work herewith reported upon.

The fundamental point in the psychology of an occupation is that it maintains a balance between the intellectual and the practical phases of experience. As an occupation it is active or motor; it finds expression through the physical organs—the eyes, hands, etc. But it also involves continual observation of materials, and continual planning and reflection, in order that the practical or executive side may be successfully carried on. Occupation as thus conceived must, therefore, be carefully distinguished from work which educates primarily for a trade. It differs because its end is in itself; in the growth that comes from the continual interplay of ideas and their embodiment in action, not in external utility.

It is possible to carry on this type of work in other than trade schools, so that the entire emphasis falls upon the manual or physical side. In such cases the work is reduced to a mere routine or custom, and its educational value is lost. This is the inevitable tendency wherever, in manual training for instance, the mastery of certain tools, or the production of certain objects, is made the primary end, and the child is not given, wherever possible, intellectual responsibility for selecting the materials and instruments that are most fit, and given an opportunity to think out his own model and plan of work, led to perceive his own errors, and find out how to correct them—that is, of course, within the range of his capacities. So far as the external result is held in view, rather than the mental and moral states and growth involved in the process of reaching the result, the work may be called manual, but cannot rightly be termed an occupation. Of course the tendency of all mere habit, routine, or custom is to result in what is unconscious and mechanical. That of occupation is to put the maximum of consciousness into whatever is done.

This enables us to interpret the stress laid (a) upon personal experimenting, planning, and reinventing in connection with the textile work, and (b) its parallelism with lines of historical development. The first requires the child to be mentally quick and alert at every point in order that he may do the outward work properly. The second enriches and deepens the work performed by saturating it with values suggested from the social life which it recapitulates.

Occupations, so considered, furnish the ideal occasions for both sense-training and discipline in thought. The weakness of ordinary lessons in observation, calculated to train the senses, is that they have no outlet beyond themselves, and hence no necessary motive. Now, in the natural life of the individual and the race there is always a reason for sense-observation. There is always some need, coming from an end to be reached, that makes one look about to discover and discriminate whatever will assist him. Normal sensations operate as clues, as aids, as stimuli, in directing activity in what has to be done; they are not ends in themselves. Separated from real needs and motives, sense-training becomes a mere gymnastic and easily degenerates into acquiring what are hardly more than mere knacks or tricks in observation, or else mere excitement of the sense organs.

The same principle applies in normal *thinking*. It also does not occur for its own sake, nor end in itself. It arises from the need of meeting some difficulty, in reflecting upon the best way of overcoming it, and thus leads to planning, to projecting mentally the result to be reached, and deciding upon the steps necessary and their serial order. This concrete logic of action long precedes the logic of pure speculation or abstract investigation, and through the mental habits that it forms is the best of preparations for the latter.

Another educational point upon which the psychology of occupations throws helpful light is the place of interest in school work. One of the objections regularly brought against giving in school work any large or positive place to the child's interest is the impossibility on such a basis of proper selection. The child, it is said, has all kinds of interests, good, bad, and indifferent. It is necessary to decide between the interests that are really important and those that are trivial; between those that are helpful and those that are harmful; between those that are transitory or mark immediate excitement, and those which endure and are permanently influential. It would seem as if we had to go beyond interest to get any basis for using interest.

Now, there can be no doubt that occupation work possesses a strong interest for the child. A glance into any school where such work is carried on will give sufficient evidence of this fact. Outside of the school, a large portion of the children's plays are simply more or less miniature and haphazard attempts at reproducing social occupations. There are certain reasons for believing that the type of interest which springs up along with these occupations is of a thoroughly healthy, permanent, and really educative sort; and that by giving a larger place to occupations we should secure an excellent, perhaps the very best, way of making an appeal to the child's spontaneous interest, and yet have, at the same time, some guaranty that we are not dealing with what is merely pleasure-giving, exciting, or transient.

In the first place, every interest grows out of some instinct or some habit that in turn is finally based upon an original instinct. It does not follow that all instincts are of equal value, or that we do not inherit many instincts which need transformation, rather than satisfaction, in order to be useful in life. But the instincts which find their conscious outlet and expression in occupation are bound to be of an exceedingly fundamental and permanent type. The activities of life are of necessity directed to bringing the materials and forces of nature under the control of our purposes;

of making them tributary to ends of life. Men have had to work in order to live. In and through their work they have mastered nature, they have protected and enriched the conditions of their own life, they have been awakened to the sense of their own powers—have been led to invent, to plan, and to rejoice in the acquisition of skill. In a rough way, all occupations may be classified as gathering about man's fundamental relations to the world in which he lives through getting food to maintain life; securing clothing and shelter to protect and ornament it, and thus, finally, to provide a permanent home in which all the higher and more spiritual interests may center. It is hardly unreasonable to suppose that interests which have such a history behind them must be of the worthy sort.

However, these interests as they develop in the child not only recapitulate past important activities of the race, but reproduce those of the child's present environment. He continually sees his elders engaged in such pursuits. He daily has to do with things which are the results of just such occupations. He comes in contact with facts that have no meaning, except in reference to them. Take these things out of the present social life and see how little would remain—and this not only on the material side, but as regards intellectual, aesthetic, and moral activities, for these are largely and necessarily bound up with occupations. The child's instinctive interests in this direction are, therefore, constantly reinforced by what he sees, feels, and hears going on around him. Suggestions along this line are continually coming to him; motives are awakened; his energies are stirred to action. Again, it is not unreasonable to suppose that interests which are touched so constantly, and on so many sides, belong to the worthy and enduring type.

In the third place, one of the objections made against the principle of interest in education is that it tends to disintegration of mental economy by constantly stirring up the child in this way or that, destroying continuity and thoroughness. But an occupation (such as the textile one herewith reported on) is of necessity a continuous thing. It lasts, not only for days, but for months and years. It represents, not a stirring of isolated and superficial energies, but rather a steady, continuous organization of power along certain general lines. The same is true, of course, of any other form of occupation, such as shopwork with tools, or as cooking. The occupations articulate a vast variety of impulses, otherwise separate and spasmodic, into a consistent skeleton with a firm backbone. It may well be doubted whether, wholly apart from some such regular and progressive modes of action, extending as cores throughout the entire school, it would be permanently safe to give the principle of "interest" any large place in school work.

VII

The Development of Attention

The subprimary or kindergarten department is undertaking the pedagogical problems growing out of an attempt to connect kindergarten work intimately with primary, and to readapt traditional materials and technique to meet present social conditions and our present physiological and psychological knowledge.

Little children have their observations and thoughts mainly directed toward people: what they do, how they behave, what they are occupied with, and what comes of it. Their interest is of a personal rather than of an objective or intellectual sort. Its intellectual counterpart is the story-form; not the task, consciously defined end, or problem—meaning by story-form something psychical, the holding together of a variety of persons, things, and incidents through a common idea that enlists feeling; not an outward relation or tale. Their minds seek wholes, varied through episode, enlivened with action and defined in salient features— there must be go, movement, the sense of use and operation—inspection of things separated from the idea by which they are carried. Analysis of isolated detail of form and structure neither appeals nor satisfies.

Material provided by existing social occupations is calculated to meet and feed this attitude. In previous years the children have been concerned with the occupations of the home, and the contact of homes with one another and with outside life. Now they may take up typical occupations of society at large—a step farther removed from the child's egoistic, self-absorbed interest, and yet dealing with something personal and something which touches him.

From the standpoint of educational theory, the following features may be noted:

1. The study of natural objects, processes, and relations is

placed in a human setting. During the year, a considerably detailed observation of seeds and their growth, of plants, woods, stones, animals, as to some phases of structure and habit, of geographical conditions of landscape, climate, arrangement of land and water, is undertaken. The pedagogical problem is to direct the child's power of observation, to nurture his sympathetic interest in characteristic traits of the world in which he lives, to afford interpreting material for later more special studies, and yet to supply a carrying medium for the variety of facts and ideas through the dominant spontaneous emotions and thoughts of the child. Hence their association with human life. Absolutely no separation is made between the "social" side of the work, its concern with people's activities and their mutual dependencies, and the "science," regard for physical facts and forces—because the conscious distinction between man and nature is the result of later reflection and abstraction, and to force it upon the child here is not only to fail to engage his whole mental energy, but to confuse and distract him. The environment is always that in which life is situated and through which it is circumstanced; and to isolate it, to make it with little children an object of observation and remark by itself, is to treat human nature inconsiderately. At last, the original open and free attitude of the mind to nature is destroyed; nature has been reduced to a mass of meaningless details.

In its emphasis upon the "concrete" and "individual," modern pedagogical theory often loses sight of the fact that the existence and presentation of an individual physical thing—a stone, an orange, a cat—is no guaranty of *concreteness*; that this is a psychological affair, whatever appeals to the mind as a whole, as a self-sufficient center of interest and attention. The reaction from this external and somewhat dead standpoint often assumes, however, that the needed clothing with human significance can come only by direct personification, and we have that continued symbolization of a plant, cloud, or rain which makes only pseudo-science possible; which, instead of generating love for nature itself, switches interest to certain sensational and emotional accompaniments, and leaves it, at last, dissipated and burnt out. And even the tendency to approach nature through the medium of literature, the pine tree through the fable of the discontented pine, etc., while recognizing the need of the human association, fails to note that there is a more straightforward road from mind to the object—direct through connection with life itself; and that the poem and story, the literary statement, have their place as reinforcements and idealizations, not as foundation stones. What is wanted, in other words, is not to fix up a connection of child mind and nature, but to give free and effective play to the connection already operating.

2. This suggests at once the practical questions that are usu-

ally discussed under the name of "correlation," questions of such interaction of the various matters studied and powers under acquisition as will avoid waste and maintain unity of mental growth. From the standpoint adopted the problem is one of differentiation rather than of correlation as ordinarily understood. The unity of life, as it presents itself to the child, binds together and carries along the different occupations, the diversity of plants, animals, and geographic conditions; drawing, modeling, games, constructive work, numerical calculations are ways of carrying certain features of it to mental and emotional satisfaction and completeness. Not much attention is paid in this year to reading and writing; but it is obvious that if this were regarded as desirable, the same principle would apply. It is the community and continuity of the subject-matter that organizes, that correlates; correlation is not through devices of instruction which the teacher employs in tying together things in themselves disconnected.

3. Two recognized demands of primary education are often, at present, not unified or are even opposed. The need of the familiar, the already experienced, as a basis for moving upon the unknown and remote, is a commonplace. The claims of the child's imagination as a factor is at least beginning to be recognized. The problem is to work these two forces together, instead of separately. The child is too often given drill upon familiar objects and ideas under the sanction of the first principle, while he is intro-

duced with equal directness to the weird, strange, and impossible
to satisfy the claims of the second. The result, it is hardly too
much to say, is a twofold failure. There is no special connection
between the unreal, the myth, the fairy tale, and the play of mental imagery. Imagination is not a matter of an impossible subject-
matter, but a constructive way of dealing with any subject-matter
under the influence of a pervading idea. The point is not to dwell
with wearisome iteration upon the familiar and under the guise
of object-lessons to keep the senses directed at material which
they have already made acquaintance with, but to enliven and
illumine the ordinary, commonplace, and homely by using it to
build up and appreciate situations previously unrealized and alien.
And this also is culture of imagination. Some writers appear to
have the impression that the child's imagination has outlet only
in myth and fairy tale of ancient time and distant place or in
weaving egregious fabrications regarding sun, moon, and stars;
and have even pleaded for a mythical investiture of all "science"
—as a way of satisfying the dominating imagination of the child.
But fortunately these things are exceptions, are intensifications,
are relaxations of the average child; not his pursuits. The John
and Jane that most of us know let their imaginations play about
the current and familiar contacts and events of life—about father
and mother and friend, about steamboats and locomotives, and
sheep and cows, about the romance of farm and forest, of sea-

shore and mountain. What is needed, in a word, is to afford occasion by which the child is moved to educe and exchange with others his store of experiences, his range of information, to make new observations correcting and extending them in order to keep his images moving, in order to find mental rest and satisfaction in definite and vivid realization of what is new and enlarging.

With the development of reflective attention come the need and the possibility of a change in the mode of the child's instruction. In the previous paragraphs we have been concerned with the direct, spontaneous attitude that marks the child till into his seventh year—his demand for new experiences and his desire to complete his partial experiences by building up images and expressing them in play. This attitude is typical of what writers call spontaneous attention, or, as some say, non-voluntary attention.

The child is simply absorbed in what he is doing; the occupation in which he is engaged lays complete hold upon him. He gives himself without reserve. Hence, while there is much energy spent, there is no *conscious* effort; while the child is intent to the point of engrossment, there is no *conscious* intention.

With the development of a sense of more remote ends, and of the need of directing acts so as to make them means for these ends (a matter discussed in the second number), we have the transition to what is termed indirect, or, as some writers prefer to say, voluntary, attention. A result is imaged, and the child attends to what is before him or what he is immediately doing because it helps to secure the result. Taken by itself, the object or the act might be indifferent or even repulsive. But because it is felt to belong to something desirable or valuable, it borrows the latter's attracting and holding power.

This is the transition to "voluntary" attention, but only the transition. The latter comes fully into being only when the child entertains results in the form of problems or questions, the solution of which he is to seek for himself. In the intervening stage (in the child from eight to, say, eleven or twelve), while the child directs a series of intervening activities on the basis of some end he wishes to reach, this end is something to be done or made, or some tangible result to be reached; the problem is a practical difficulty, rather than an intellectual question. But with growing power the child can conceive of the end as something to be found out, discovered; and can control his acts and images so as to help in the inquiry and solution. This is reflective attention proper.

In history work there is change from the story and biography form, from discussion of questions that arise, to the formulation of questions. Points about which difference of opinion is possible, matters upon which experience, reflection, etc., can be brought to bear, are always coming up in history. But to use the discussion to develop this matter of doubt and difference into a definite problem, to bring the child to feel just what the difficulty is, and then throw him upon his own resources in looking up material bearing upon the point, and upon his judgment in bringing it to bear, or getting a solution, is a marked intellectual advance. So in the science there is a change from the practical attitude of making and using cameras to the consideration of the problems intellectually involved in this—to principles of light, angular measurements, etc., which give the theory or explanation of the practice.

In general, this growth is a natural process. But the proper recognition and use of it is perhaps the most serious problem in instruction upon the intellectual side. A person who has gained the power of reflective attention, the power to hold problems, questions, before the mind, *is* in so far, intellectually speaking, educated. He has mental discipline—power *of* the mind and *for* the mind. Without this the mind remains at the mercy of custom and external suggestions. Some of the difficulties may be barely indicated by referring to an error that almost dominates instruction of the usual type. Too often it is assumed that attention can be given directly to any subject-matter, if only the proper will or disposition be at hand, failure being regarded as a sign of unwillingness or indocility. Lessons in arithmetic, geography, and grammar are put before the child, and he is told to attend in order to learn. But excepting as there is some question, some doubt, present in the mind as a basis for this attention, *reflective* attention is

kids won't pay attention unless they have a genuine interest in a problem and can relate it to earlier learning

[handwritten margin note: should a teacher attempt to illustrate something's relevance/interest for st., or wait for them to ask the questions/make the connections themselves in order to make the learning truly authentic]

impossible. If there is sufficient *intrinsic* interest in the material, there will be direct or spontaneous attention, which is excellent so far as it goes, but which merely of itself does not give power of thought or internal mental control. If there is not an inherent attracting power in the material, then (according to his temperament and training, and the precedents and expectations of the school) the teacher will either attempt to surround the material with foreign attractiveness, making a bid or offering a bribe for attention by "making the lesson interesting"; or else will resort to counterirritants (low marks, threats of non-promotion, staying after school, personal disapprobation, expressed in a great variety of ways, naggings, continuous calling upon the child to "pay attention," etc.); or, probably, will use some of both means.

But (1) the attention thus gained is never more than partial, or divided; and (2) it always remains dependent upon something external—hence, when the attraction ceases or the pressure lets up, there is little or no gain in inner or intellectual control. And (3) such attention is always for the sake of "learning," i.e., *memorizing ready-made answers to possible questions to be put by another.* True, reflective attention, on the other hand, always involves judging, reasoning, deliberation; it means that the child has a question of his own and is actively engaged in seeking and selecting relevant material with which to answer it, considering the bearings and relations of this material—the kind of solution

148

[handwritten note at bottom: should st. ever be required to learn and persevere through something they don't find interesting and/or engaging?]

it calls for. The problem is one's own; hence also the impetus, the stimulus to attention, is one's own; hence also the training secured is one's own—it is discipline, or gain in power of control; that is, a *habit* of considering problems.

It is hardly too much to say that in the traditional education so much stress has been laid upon the presentation to the child of ready-made material (books, object-lessons, teacher's talks, etc.), and the child has been so almost exclusively held to bare responsibility for reciting upon this ready-made material, that there has been only accidental occasion and motive for developing reflective attention. Next to no consideration has been paid to the fundamental necessity—leading the child to realize a problem as his own, so that he is self-induced to attend in order to find out its answer. So completely have the conditions for securing this self-putting of problems been neglected that the very idea of voluntary attention has been radically perverted. It is regarded as measured by unwilling effort—as activity called out by foreign, and so repulsive, material under conditions of strain, instead of as self-initiated effort. "Voluntary" is treated as meaning the reluctant and disagreeable instead of the free, the self-directed, through personal interest, insight, and power.

VIII
The Aim of History in Elementary Education

If history be regarded as just the record of the past, it is hard to see any grounds for claiming that it should play any large rôle in the curriculum of elementary education. The past is the past, and the dead may be safely left to bury its dead. There are too many urgent demands in the present, too many calls over the threshold of the future, to permit the child to become deeply immersed in what is forever gone by. Not so when history is considered as an account of the forces and forms of social life. Social life we have always with us; the distinction of past and present is indifferent to it. Whether it was lived just here or just there is a matter of slight moment. It is life for all that; it shows the motives which draw men together and push them apart, and depicts what is desirable and what is hurtful. Whatever history may be for the scientific historian, for the educator it must be an indirect sociology—a study of society which lays bare its process of becoming and its modes of organization. Existing society is both too complex and too close to the child to be studied. He finds no clues into its labyrinth of detail and can mount no eminence whence to get a perspective of arrangement.

If the aim of historical instruction is to enable the child to appreciate the values of social life, to see in imagination the forces which favor and allow men's effective co-operation with one another, to understand the sorts of character that help on and that hold back, the essential thing in its presentation is to make it moving, dynamic. History must be presented, not as an accumulation of results or effects, a mere statement of what happened, but as a forceful, acting thing. The motives—that is, the motors—must stand out. To study history is not to amass information, but to use information in constructing a vivid picture of how and why men did thus and so; achieved their successes and came to their failures.

151

When history is conceived as dynamic, as moving, its economic and industrial aspects are emphasized. These are but technical terms which express the problem with which humanity is unceasingly engaged; how to live, how to master and use nature so as to make it tributary to the enrichment of human life. The great advances in civilization have come through those manifestations of intelligence which have lifted man from his precarious subjection to nature, and revealed to him how he may make its forces co-operate with his own purposes. The social world in which the child now lives is so rich and full that it is not easy to see how much it cost, how much effort and thought lie back of it. Man has a tremendous equipment ready at hand. The child may be led to translate these ready-made resources into fluid terms; he may be led to see man face to face with nature, without inherited capital, without tools, without manufactured materials. And, step by step, he may follow the processes by which man recognized the needs of his situation, thought out the weapons and instruments that enable him to cope with them; and may learn how these new resources opened new horizons of growth and created new problems. The industrial history of man is not a materialistic or merely utilitarian affair. It is a matter of intelligence. Its record is the record of how man learned to think, to think to some effect, to transform the conditions of life so that life itself became a different thing. It is an ethical record as well; the account

152

of the conditions which men have patiently wrought out to serve their ends.

The question of how human beings live, indeed, represents the dominant interest with which the child approaches historic material. It is this point of view which brings those who worked in the past close to the beings with whom he is daily associated, and confers upon him the gift of sympathetic penetration.

The child who is interested in the way in which men lived, the tools they had to do with, the new inventions they made, the transformations of life that arose from the power and leisure thus gained, is eager to repeat like processes in his own action, to remake utensils, to reproduce processes, to rehandle materials. Since he understands their problems and their successes only by seeing what obstacles and what resources they had from nature, the child is interested in field and forest, ocean and mountain, plant and animal. By building up a conception of the natural environment in which lived the people he is studying, he gets his hold upon their lives. This reproduction he cannot make excepting as he gains acquaintance with the natural forces and forms with which he is himself surrounded. The interest in history gives a more human coloring, a wider significance, to his own study of nature. His knowledge of nature lends point and accuracy to his study of history. This is the natural "correlation" of history and science.

This same end, a deepening appreciation of social life, decides the place of the biographic element in historical instruction. That historical material appeals to the child most completely and vividly when presented in individual form, when summed up in the lives and deeds of some heroic character, there can be no doubt. Yet it is possible to use biographies so that they become a collection of mere stories, interesting, possibly, to the point of sensationalism, but yet bringing the child no nearer to comprehension of social life. This happens when the individual who is the hero of the tale is isolated from his social environment; when the child is not brought to feel the social situations which evoked his acts and the social progress to which his deeds contributed. If biography is presented as a dramatic summary of social needs and achievements, if the child's imagination pictures the social defects and problems that clamored for the man and the ways in which the individual met the emergency, then the biography is an organ of social study.

A consciousness of the social aim of history prevents any tendency to swamp history in myth, fairy story, and merely literary renderings. I cannot avoid the feeling that much as the Herbartian school has done to enrich the elementary curriculum in the direction of history, it has often inverted the true relationship existing between history and literature. In a certain sense the motif of American colonial history and of De Foe's *Robinson*

Crusoe are the same. Both represent man who has achieved civilization, who has attained a certain maturity of thought, who has developed ideals and means of action, but is suddenly thrown back upon his own resources, having to cope with a raw and often hostile nature, and to regain success by sheer intelligence, energy, and persistence of character. But when *Robinson Crusoe* supplies the material for the curriculum of the third- or fourth-grade child, are we not putting the cart before the horse? Why not give the child the reality with its much larger sweep, its intenser forces, its more vivid and lasting value for life, using the *Robinson Crusoe* as an imaginative idealization in a particular case of the same sort of problems and activities? Again, whatever may be the worth of the study of savage life in general, and of the North American Indians in particular, why should that be approached circuitously through the medium of *Hiawatha*, instead of at first hand? employing indeed the poem to furnish the idealized and culminating touches to a series of conditions and struggles which the child has previously realized in more specific form. Either the life of the Indian presents some permanent questions and factors in social life, or it has next to no place in a scheme of instruction. If it has such a value, this should be made to stand out on its own account, instead of being lost in the very refinement and beauty of a purely literary presentation.

The same end, the understanding of character and social relations in their natural dependence, enables us, I think, to decide upon the importance to be attached to chronological order in historical instruction. Considerable stress has of late been laid upon the supposed necessity of following the development of civilization through the successive steps in which it actually took place—beginning with the valleys of the Euphrates and the Nile, and coming on down through Greece, Rome, etc. The point urged is that the present depends upon the past and each phase of the past upon a prior past.

We are here introduced to a conflict between the logical and psychological interpretation of history. If the aim be an appreciation of what social life is and how it goes on, then, certainly, the child must deal with what is near in spirit, not with the remote. The difficulty with the Babylonian or Egyptian life is not so much its remoteness in time as its remoteness from the present interests and aims of social life. It does not simplify enough and does not generalize enough or, at least, it does not do so in the right way. It does it by omission of what is significant now, rather than by presenting these factors arranged on a lower scale. Its salient features are hard to get at and to understand, even by the specialist. It undoubtedly presents factors which contributed to later life, and which modified the course of events in the stream of time. But the child has not arrived at a point where he can appreciate abstract causes and specialized contributions. What he needs is a picture of typical relations, conditions, and activities. In this respect, there is much of prehistoric life which is much closer to him than the complicated and artificial life of Babylon or of Egypt. When a child is capable of appreciating institutions, he is capable of seeing what special institutional idea each historic nation stands for, and what factor it has contributed to the present complex of institutions. But this period arrives only when the child is beginning to be capable of abstracting causes in other realms as well; in other words, when he is approaching the time of secondary education.

In this general scheme three periods or phases are recognized: first comes the generalized and simplified history—history which is hardly history at all in the local or chronological sense, but which aims at giving the child insight into, and sympathy with, a variety of social activities. This period includes the work of the six-year-old children in studying typical occupations of people in the country and city at present; of the seven-year-old children in working out the evolution of inventions and their effects upon life, and of the eight-year-old children in dealing with the great movements of migration, exploration, and discovery which have brought the whole round world into human ken. The work of the first two years is evidently quite independent of any particular people or any particular person—that is, of historical data in the strict sense of the term. At the same time, plenty of scope is provided through dramatization for the introduction of the individual factor. The account of the great explorers and the discoverers serves to make the transition to what is local and specific, that which depends upon certain specified persons who lived at certain specified places and times.

This introduces us to the second period where local conditions and the definite activities of particular bodies of people become prominent—corresponding to the child's growth in power of dealing with limited and positive fact. Since Chicago, since the United States, are localities with which the child can, by the nature of the case, most effectively deal, the material of the next three years is derived directly and indirectly from this source. Here, again, the third year is a transitional year, taking up the connections of American life with European. By this time the child should be ready to deal, not with social life in general, or even with the social life with which he is most familiar, but with certain thoroughly differentiated and, so to speak, peculiar types of social life; with the special significance of each and the particular contribution it has made to the whole world-history. Accordingly, in the next period the chronological order is followed, beginning with the ancient world about the Mediterranean and coming down again through European history to the peculiar and differentiating factors of American history.

The program is not presented as the only one meeting the

problem, but as a contribution; the outcome, not of thought, but of considerable experimenting and shifting of subjects from year to year, to the problem of giving material which takes vital hold upon the child and at the same time leads on, step by step, to more thorough and accurate knowledge of both the principles and facts of social life, and makes a preparation for later specialized historic studies.

POSTSCRIPT:
THREE YEARS OF THE
UNIVERSITY ELEMENTARY
SCHOOL

Three Years of the University Elementary School

The school was started the first week in January, three years ago. I shall try this afternoon to give a brief statement of the ideas and problems that were in mind when the experiment was started, and a sketch of the development of the work since that time. We began in a small house in Fifty-seventh street, with fifteen children. We

Stenographic report of a talk by John Dewey at a meeting of the Parents' Association of the University Elementary School, February, 1899; somewhat revised.

found ourselves the next year with twenty-five children in Kimbark avenue, and then moved in January to Rosalie court, the larger quarters enabling us to take forty children. The next year the numbers increased to sixty, the school remaining at Rosalie court. This year we have had ninety-five on the roll at one time, and are located at 5412 Ellis avenue, where we hope to stay till we have a building and grounds of our own.

The children during the first year of the school were between the ages of six and nine. Now their ages range between four and thirteen—the members of the oldest group being in their thirteenth year. This is the first year that we have children under six, and this has been made possible through the liberality of friends in Honolulu, H.I., who are building up there a memorial kindergarten along the same lines.

The expenses of the school during the first year, of two terms only, were between $1,300 and $1,400. The expenses this year will be about $12,000. Of this amount $5,500 will come from tuitions; $5,000 has been given by friends interested in the school, and there remains about $1,500 yet to be raised for the conduct of the school. This is an indication of the increase of expenses. The average expense per pupil is about the same since the start, *i.e.*, $120 per child per school year. Relatively speaking, this year the expenses of the school took something of a jump, through the expense of moving to a new building, and the repairs and changes there necessary. An increase in the staff of teachers has also enlarged the work as well as the debits of the school. Next year (1899–1900) we hope to have about 120 children, and apparently the expenses will be about $2,500 more than this. Of this amount $2,000 will be met by the increase in tuition from the pupils. The cost of a child to the school, $120 a year, is precisely the tuition charged by the University for students and is double the average tuition charged by the school. But it is not expected that the University tuition will come anywhere near meeting the expense involved there. One reason for not increasing the tuition here, even if it were advisable for other reasons, is that it is well to emphasize, from an educational point of view, that elementary as well as advanced education requires endowment. There is every reason why money should be spent freely for the organization and maintenance of foundation work in education as well as for the later stages.

The elementary school has had from the outset two sides: one, the obvious one of instruction of the children who have been intrusted to it; the other, relationship to the University, since the school is under the charge, and forms a part of the pedagogical work of the University.

When the school was started, there were certain ideas in mind— perhaps it would be better to say questions and problems; certain points which it seemed worth while to test. If you will permit one personal word, I should like to say that it is sometimes thought that the school started out with a number of ready-made principles and ideas which were to be put into practice at once. It has been popularly assumed that I am the author of these ready-made ideas and principles which were to go into execution. I take this opportunity to say that the educational conduct of the school, as well as its administration, the selection of subject-matter, and the working out of the course of study, as well as actual instruction of children, have been almost entirely in the hands of the teachers of the school; and that there has been a gradual development of the educational principles and methods involved, not a fixed equipment. The teachers started with question marks, rather than with fixed rules, and if any answers have been reached, it is the teachers in the school who have supplied them. We started upon the whole with four such questions, or problems:

I. What can be done, and how can it be done, to bring the school into closer relation with the home and neighborhood life—instead of having the school a place where the child comes solely to learn certain lessons? What can be done to break down the barriers which have unfortunately come to separate the school life from the rest of the everyday life of the child? This does not mean, as it is sometimes, perhaps, interpreted to mean, that the child should simply take up in the school things already experienced at home and study them, but that, so far as possible, the child shall have the same attitude and point of view in the school as in the home; that he shall find the same interest in going to school, and in there doing things worth doing for their own sake, that he finds in the plays and occupations which busy him in his home and neighborhood life. It means, again, that the motives which keep the child at work and growing at home shall be used in the school, so that he shall not have to acquire another set of principles of actions belonging only to the school—separate from those of the home. It is a question of the unity of the child's experience, of its actuating motives and aims, not of amusing or even interesting the child.

2. What can be done in the way of introducing subject-matter in history and science and art, that shall have a positive value and real significance in the child's own life; that shall represent, even to the youngest children, something worthy of attainment in skill or knowledge; as much so to the little pupil as are the studies of the high-school or college student to him? You know what the traditional curriculum of the first few years is, even though many modifications have been made. Some statistics have been collected showing that 75 or 80 per cent. of the first three years of a child in school are spent upon the form—not the substance—of learning, the mastering of the symbols of reading, writing, and arithmetic. There is not much positive nutriment in this. Its purpose is important—is necessary—but it does not represent the same kind of increase in a child's intellectual and moral experience that is represented by positive truth of history and nature, or by added insight into reality and

167

beauty. One thing, then, we wanted to find out is how much can be given a child that is really worth his while to get, in knowledge of the world about him, of the forces in the world, of historical and social growth, and in capacity to express himself in a variety of artistic forms. From the strictly educational side this has been the chief problem of the school. It is along this line that we hope to make our chief contribution to education in general; we hope, that is, to work out and publish a positive body of subject-matter which may be generally available.

3. How can instruction in these formal, symbolic branches—the mastering of the ability to read, write, and use figures intelligently—be carried on with everyday experience and occupation as their background and in definite relations to other studies of more inherent content, and be carried on in such a way that the child shall feel their necessity through their connection with subjects which appeal to him on their own account? If this can be accomplished, he will have a vital motive for getting the technical capacity. It is not meant, as has been sometimes jocosely stated, that the child learn to bake and sew at school, and to read, write, and figure at home. It is intended that these formal subjects shall not be presented in such large doses at first as to be the exclusive objects of attention, and that the child shall be led by that which he is doing to feel the need for acquiring skill in the use of symbols and the immediate power they give. In any school, if the child realizes the motive for the use and

application of number and language he has taken the longest step toward securing the power; and he can realize the motive only as he has some particular—not some general and remote—use for the symbols.

4. Individual attention. This is secured by small groupings— eight or ten in a class—and a large number of teachers supervising systematically the intellectual needs and attainments and physical well-being and growth of the child. To secure this we have now 135 hours of instructors' time per week, that is, the time of nine teachers for three hours per day, or one teacher per group. It requires but a few words to make this statement about attention to individual powers and needs, and yet the whole of the school's aims and methods, moral, physical, intellectual, are bound up in it.

I think these four points present a fair statement of what we have set out to discover. The school is often called an experimental school, and in one sense that is the proper name. I do not like to use it too much, for fear parents will think we are experimenting upon the children, and that they naturally object to. But it is an experimental school—at least I hope so—with reference to education and educational problems. We have attempted to find out by trying, by doing—not alone by discussion and theorizing—*whether* these problems may be worked out, and *how* they may be worked out.

Next a few words about the means that have been used in the school in order to test these four questions, and to supply their answers, and first as to the place given to hand-work of different kinds in the school. There are three main lines regularly pursued: (*a*) the shop-work with woods and tools, (*b*) cooking work, and (*c*) work with textiles—sewing and weaving. Of course, there is other hand-work in connection with science, as science is largely of an experimental nature. It is a fact that may not have come to your attention that a large part of the best and most advanced scientific work involves a great deal of manual skill, the training of the hand and eye. It is impossible for one to be a first-class worker in science without this training in manipulation, and in handling apparatus and materials. In connection with the history work, especially with the younger children, hand-work is brought in in the way of making implements, weapons, tools, etc. Of course, the art work is another side— drawing, painting, and modeling. Logically, perhaps, the gymnasium work does not come in here, but as a means of developing moral and intellectual control through the medium of the body it certainly does. The children have one-half hour per day of this form of physical exercise. Along this line we have found that hand-work, in large variety and amount, is the most easy and natural method of keeping up the same attitude of the child in and out of the school. The child gets the largest part of his acquisitions through his bodily activities, until he learns to work systematically with the intellect. That is the purpose of this work in the school, to direct these activities, to systematize and organize them, so that they shall not be as haphazard and as wandering as they are outside of school. The problem of making these forms of practical activity work continuously and definitely together, leading from one factor of skill to another, from one intellectual difficulty to another, has been one of the most difficult, and at the same time one in which we have been most successful. The various kinds of work, carpentry, cooking, sewing, and weaving, are selected as involving different kinds of skill, and demanding different types of intellectual attitude on the part of the child, and because they represent some of the most important activities of the everyday outside world: the question of living under shelter, of daily food and clothing, of the home, of personal movement and exchange of goods. He gets also the training of sense organs, of touch, of sight, and the ability to coördinate eye and hand. He gets healthy exercise; for the child demands a much larger amount of physical activity than the formal program of the ordinary school permits. There is also a continual appeal to memory, to judgment, in adapting ends to means, a training in habits of order, industry, and neatness in the care of the tools and utensils, and in doing things in a systematic, instead of a haphazard, way. Then, again, these practical occupations make a background, especially in the earlier groups, for the later studies. The children get a good deal of chemistry in connection with cooking, of number work and geometrical principles in carpentry, and a good deal of geography in connection with their theoretical work in weaving and sewing. History also

171

comes in with the origin and growth of various inventions, and their effects upon social life and political organization.

Perhaps more attention, upon the whole, has been given to our second point, that of positive subject-matter, than to any one other thing. On the history side the curriculum is now fairly well worked out. The younger children begin with the home and occupations of the home. In the sixth year the intention is that the children should study occupations outside the home, the larger social industries— farming, mining, lumber, etc.—that they may see the complex and various social industries on which life depends, while incidentally they investigate the use of the various materials—woods, metals, and the processes applied—thus getting a beginning of scientific study. The next year is given to the historical development of industry and invention—starting with man as a savage and carrying him through the typical phases of his progress upward, until the iron age is reached and man begins to enter upon a civilized career. The object of the study of primitive life is not to keep the child interested in lower and relatively savage stages, but to show him the steps of pro- gress and development, especially along the line of invention, by which man was led into civilization. There is a certain nearness, after all, in the child to primitive forms of life. They are much more simple than existing institutions. By throwing the emphasis upon the progress of man, and upon the way advance has been made, we hope to avoid the objections that hold against paying too much attention to the crudities and distracting excitements of savage life.

The next two or three years, *i.e.*, the fourth and fifth grades, and perhaps the sixth, will be devoted to American history. It is then that history, properly speaking, begins, as the study of primitive life can hardly be so called.

Then comes Greek history and Roman, in the regular chronological order, each year having its own work planned with reference to what has come before and after.

The science work was more difficult to arrange and systematize, because there was so little to follow—so little that has been already done in an organized way. We are now at work upon a program,[1] and I shall not speak in detail about it. The first two or three years cultivate the children's powers of observation, lead them to sympathetic interest in the habits of plants and animals, and to look at things with reference to their uses. Then the center of the work becomes geographical—the study of the earth, as the most central thing. From this almost all the work grows out, and to it the work goes back. Another standpoint in the science work is that of the application of natural forces to the service of man through machines. Last year a good deal of work was done in electricity (and will be

[1]This year's program is published in the *Elementary School Record*. Address The University of Chicago Press for particulars.

repeated this year), based on the telegraph and telephone—taking up the things that can easily be grasped.

In mechanics they have studied locks and clocks with reference to the adaptation of the various parts of the machinery. All this work makes a most excellent basis for more formal physics later on. Cooking gives opportunity for getting a great many ideas of heat and water, and of their effects. The scientific work taken up in the school differs mainly from that of other schools in having the experimental part—physics and chemistry—emphasized, and is not confined simply to nature study—the study of plants and animals. Not that the latter is less valuable, but that we find it possible to introduce the physical aspects from the first.

If I do not spend a large amount of time in speaking of the music and art work, it is not because they are not considered valuable and important—certainly as much so as any other work done in the school, not only in the development of the child's moral and aesthetic nature, but also from a strictly intellectual point of view. I know of no work in the school that better develops the power of attention, the habit of observation and of consecutiveness, of seeing parts in relation to a whole.

I shall now say a few words about the administrative side of the school. At the outset we mixed up the children of different ages and attainments as much as possible, believing there were mental advantages in the give-and-take thus secured, as well as the moral advantages in having the older assume certain responsibilities in the care of the younger. As the school grew, it became necessary to abandon the method, and to group the children with reference to their common capacities. These groupings, however, are based, not on ability to read and write, but upon similarity of mental attitude and interest, and upon general intellectual capacity and mental alertness. There are ways in which we are still trying to carry out the idea of mixing up the children, that we may not build the rigid stepladder system of the "graded" school. One step in this direction is having the children move about and come in contact with different teachers. While there are difficulties and evils connected with this, I think one of the most useful things in the school is that children come into intimate relation with a number of different personalities. The children also meet in general assemblies—for singing, and for the report of the whole school work as read by members of the different groups. The older children are also given a half hour a week in which to join some of the younger groups, and, if possible, as in hand-work, enter into the work of the younger children. In various ways we are attempting to keep a family spirit throughout the school, and not the feeling of isolated classes and grades.

The organization of the teaching force has gradually become departmental, as the needs of the work have indicated its chief branches. So we now have recognized divisions of Science, History, Domestic or Household Arts, Manual Training in the limited sense (wood and metals), Music, Art (that is, drawing, water colors, clay modeling, etc.), and Gymnasium. As the work goes on into the secondary period, the languages and mathematics will also of necessity assume a more differentiated and distinct position. As it is sometimes said that correlated or thoroughly harmonized work cannot be secured upon this basis, I am happy to say that our experience shows positively that there are no intrinsic difficulties. Through common devotion to the best development of the child, through common loyalty to the main aims and methods of the school, our teachers have demonstrated that in education, as in business, the best organization is secured through proper regard for natural divisions of labor, interest, and training. The child secures the advantage in discipline and knowledge of contact with experts in each line, while the individual teachers serve the common thought in diverse ways, thus multiplying and re-inforcing it.

Upon the moral side, that of so-called discipline and order, where the work of the University Elementary School has perhaps suffered most from misunderstanding and misrepresentation, I shall say only that our ideal has been, and continues to be, that of the best form of family life, rather than that of a rigid graded school. In the latter, the large number of children under the care of a single teacher, and the very limited number of modes of activity open to the pupils, have made necessary certain fixed and somewhat external forms of "keeping order." It would be very stupid to copy these, under the changed conditions of our school, its small groups permitting and requiring the most intimate personal acquaintance of child and teacher, and its great variety of forms of work, with their differing adaptations to the needs of different children. If we have permitted to our children more than the usual amount of freedom, it has not been in order to relax or decrease real discipline, but because under our particular conditions larger and less artificial responsibilities could thus be required of the children, and their entire development of body and spirit be more harmonious and complete. And I am confident that the parents who have intrusted their children to us for any length of time will agree in saying that, while the children like, or love, to come to school, yet work, and not amusement, has been the spirit and teaching of the school; and that this freedom has been granted under such conditions of intelligent and sympathetic oversight as to be a means of upbuilding and strengthening character.

At the end of three years, then, we are not afraid to say that some of our original questions have secured affirmative answers. The increase of our children from fifteen to almost one hundred, along with a practical doubling of fees, has shown that parents are ready for a form of education that makes individual growth its sole controlling aim. The presence of an organized corps of instructors demonstrates that thoroughly educated teachers are ready to bring to elementary education the same resources of training, knowledge, and skill that have long been at the command of higher education. The everyday work of the school shows that children can live in school as out of it, and yet grow daily in wisdom, kindness, and the spirit of obedience—that learning may, even with little children, lay hold upon the substance of truth that nourishes the spirit, and yet the forms of knowledge be observed and cultivated; and that growth may be genuine and thorough, and yet a delight.

THE CHILD AND THE
CURRICULUM

The Child and the Curriculum

Profound differences in theory are never gratuitous or invented. They grow out of conflicting elements in a genuine problem—a problem which is genuine just because the elements, taken as they stand, are conflicting. Any significant problem involves conditions that for the moment contradict each other. Solution comes only by getting away from the meaning of terms that is already fixed upon and coming to see the conditions from another point of view, and hence in a fresh light. But this reconstruction means travail of thought. Easier than thinking with surrender of already formed ideas and detachment from facts already learned is just to stick by what is already said, looking about for something with which to buttress it against attack.

Thus sects arise: schools of opinion. Each selects that set of conditions that appeals to it; and then erects them into a complete and independent truth, instead of treating them as a factor in a problem, needing adjustment.

The fundamental factors in the educative process are an immature, undeveloped being; and certain social aims, meanings, values incarnate in the matured experience of the adult. The educative process is the due interaction of these forces. Such a conception of each in relation to the other as facilitates completest and freest interaction is the essence of educational theory.

But here comes the effort of thought. It is easier to see the conditions in their separateness, to insist upon one at the expense of the other, to make antagonists of them, than to discover a reality to which each belongs. The easy thing is to seize upon something in the nature of the child, or upon something in the developed consciousness of the adult, and insist upon *that* as the key to the whole problem. When this happens a really serious practical problem—that of interaction—is transformed into an unreal, and hence insoluble, theoretic problem. Instead of seeing the educative steadily and as a whole, we see conflicting terms. We get the case of the child *vs.* the curriculum; of the individual nature *vs.* social culture. Below all other divisions in pedagogic opinion lies this opposition.

The child lives in a somewhat narrow world of personal contacts. Things hardly come within his experience unless they touch, intimately and obviously, his own well-being, or that of his family and friends. His world is a world of persons with their personal interests, rather than a realm of facts and laws. Not truth, in the sense of conformity to external fact, but affection and sympathy, is its keynote. As against this, the course of study met in the school presents material stretching back indefinitely in time, and extending outward indefinitely into space. The child is taken out of his familiar physical environment, hardly more than a square mile or so in area, into the wide world—yes, and even to the bounds of the solar system. His little span of personal memory and tradition is overlaid with the long centuries of the history of all peoples.

Again, the child's life is an integral, a total one. He passes quickly and readily from one topic to another, as from one spot to another, but is not conscious of transition or break. There is no conscious isolation, hardly conscious distinction. The things that occupy him are held together by the unity of the personal and social interests which his life carries along. Whatever is

183

uppermost in his mind constitutes to him, for the time being, the whole universe. That universe is fluid and fluent; its contents dissolve and re-form with amazing rapidity. But, after all, it is the child's own world. It has the unity and completeness of his own life. He goes to school, and various studies divide and fractionize the world for him. Geography selects, it abstracts and analyzes one set of facts, and from one particular point of view. Arithmetic is another division, grammar another department, and so on indefinitely.

Again, in school each of these subjects is classified. Facts are torn away from their original place in experience and rearranged with reference to some general principle. Classification is not a matter of child experience; things do not come to the individual pigeonholed. The vital ties of affection, the connecting bonds of activity, hold together the variety of his personal experiences. The adult mind is so familiar with the notion of logically ordered facts that it does not recognize—it cannot realize—the amount of separating and reformulating which the facts of direct experience have to undergo before they can appear as a "study," or branch of learning. A principle, for the intellect, has had to be distinguished and defined; facts have had to be interpreted in relation to this principle, not as they are in themselves. They have had to be regathered about a new center which is wholly abstract and ideal. All this means a development of a special intellectual interest. It means ability to view facts impartially and objectively; that is, without reference to their place and meaning in one's own experience. It means capacity to analyze and to synthesize. It means highly matured intellectual habits and the command of a definite technique and apparatus of scientific inquiry. The studies as classified are the product, in a word, of the science of the ages, not of the experience of the child.

These apparent deviations and differences between child and curriculum might be almost indefinitely widened. But we have here sufficiently fundamental divergences: first, the narrow but personal world of the child against the impersonal but infinitely extended world of space and time; second, the unity, the single wholeheartedness of the child's life, and the specializations and divisions of the curriculum; third, an abstract principle of logical classification and arrangement, and the practical and emotional bonds of child life.

From these elements of conflict grow up different educational sects. One school fixes its attention upon the importance of the subject-matter of the curriculum as compared with the contents of the child's own experience. It is as if they said: Is life petty, narrow, and crude? Then studies reveal the great, wide universe with all its fulness and complexity of meaning. Is the life of the child egoistic, self-centered, impulsive? Then in these studies is found an objective universe of truth, law, and order. Is his experience confused, vague, uncertain, at the mercy of the moment's caprice and circumstance? Then studies introduce a world arranged on the basis of eternal and general truth; a world where all is measured and defined. Hence the moral: ignore and minimize the child's individual peculiarities, whims, and experiences. They are what we need to get away from. They are to be obscured or eliminated. As educators our work is precisely to substitute for these superficial and casual affairs stable and well-ordered realities; and these are found in studies and lessons.

Subdivide each topic into studies; each study into lessons; each lesson into specific facts and formulae. Let the child proceed step by step to master each one of these separate parts, and at last he will have covered the entire ground. The road which looks so long when viewed in its entirety is easily traveled, considered as a series of particular steps. Thus emphasis is put upon the logical subdivisions and consecutions of the subject-matter. Problems of instruction are problems of procuring texts giving logical parts and sequences, and of presenting these portions in class in a similar definite and graded way. Subject-matter furnishes the end, and it determines method. The child is simply the immature being who is to be matured; he is the superficial being who is to be deepened; his is narrow experience which is to be widened. It is his to receive, to accept. His part is fulfilled when he is ductile and docile.

Not so, says the other sect. The child is the starting-point, the center, and the end. His development, his growth, is the ideal. It alone furnishes the standard. To the growth of the child all studies are subservient; they are instruments valued as they serve the needs of growth. Personality, character, is more than subject-matter. Not knowledge or information, but self-realization, is the goal. To possess all the world of knowledge and lose one's own self is as awful a fate in education as in religion. Moreover, subject-matter never can be got into the child from without. Learning is active. It involves reaching out of the mind. It involves organic assimilation starting from within. Literally, we must take our stand with the child and our departure from him. It is he and not the subject-matter which determines both quality and quantity of learning.

The only significant method is the method of the mind as it reaches out and assimilates. Subject-matter is but spiritual food, possible nutritive material. It cannot digest itself; it cannot of its own accord turn into bone and muscle and blood. The source of whatever is dead, mechanical, and formal in schools is found precisely in the subordination of the life and experience of the child to the curriculum. It is because of this that "study" has become a synonym for what is irksome, and a lesson identical with a task.

This fundamental opposition of child and curriculum set up by these two modes of doctrine can be duplicated in a series of

187

other terms. "Discipline" is the watchword of those who magnify the course of study; "interest" that of those who blazon "The Child" upon their banner. The standpoint of the former is logical; that of the latter psychological. The first emphasizes the necessity of adequate training and scholarship on the part of the teacher; the latter that of need of sympathy with the child, and knowledge of his natural instincts. "Guidance and control" are the catchwords of one school; "freedom and initiative" of the other. Law is asserted here; spontaneity proclaimed there. The old, the conservation of what has been achieved in the pain and toil of the ages, is dear to the one; the new, change, progress, wins the affection of the other. Inertness and routine, chaos and anarchism, are accusations bandied back and forth. Neglect of the sacred authority of duty is charged by one side, only to be met by counter-charges of suppression of individuality through tyrannical despotism.

Such oppositions are rarely carried to their logical conclusion. Common-sense recoils at the extreme character of these results. They are left to theorists, while common-sense vibrates back and forward in a maze of inconsistent compromise. The need of getting theory and practical common-sense into closer connection suggests a return to our original thesis: that we have here conditions which are necessarily related to each other in the educative process, since this is precisely one of interaction and adjustment.

What, then, is the problem? It is just to get rid of the prejudicial notion that there is some gap in kind (as distinct from degree) between the child's experience and the various forms of subject-matter that make up the course of study. From the side of the child, it is a question of seeing how his experience already contains within itself elements—facts and truths—of just the same sort as those entering into the formulated study; and, what is of more importance, of how it contains within itself the attitudes, the motives, and the interests which have operated in developing and organizing the subject-matter to the plane which it now occupies. From the side of the studies, it is a question of interpreting them as outgrowths of forces operating in the child's life, and of discovering the steps that intervene between the child's present experience and their richer maturity.

Abandon the notion of subject-matter as something fixed and ready-made in itself, outside the child's experience; cease thinking of the child's experience as also something hard and fast; see it as something fluent, embryonic, vital; and we realize that the child and the curriculum are simply two limits which define a single process. Just as two points define a straight line, so the present standpoint of the child and the facts and truths of studies define instruction. It is continuous reconstruction, moving from the child's present experience out into that represented by the organized bodies of truth that we call studies.

On the face of it, the various studies, arithmetic, geography, language, botany, etc., are themselves experience—they are that of the race. They embody the cumulative outcome of the efforts, the strivings, and the successes of the human race generation after generation. They present this, not as a mere accumulation, not as a miscellaneous heap of separate bits of experience, but in some organized and systematized way—that is, as reflectively formulated.

Hence, the facts and truths that enter into the child's present experience, and those contained in the subject-matter of studies, are the initial and final terms of one reality. To oppose one to the other is to oppose the infancy and maturity of the same growing life; it is to set the moving tendency and the final result of the same process over against each other; it is to hold that the nature and the destiny of the child war with each other.

If such be the case, the problem of the relation of the child and the curriculum presents itself in this guise: Of what use, educationally speaking, is it to be able to see the end in the beginning? How does it assist us in dealing with the early stages of growth to be able to anticipate its later phases? The studies, as we have agreed, represent the possibilities of development inherent in the child's immediate crude experience. But, after all, they are not parts of that present and immediate life. Why, then, or how, make account of them?

Asking such a question suggests its own answer. To see the outcome is to know in what direction the present experience is moving, provided it move normally and soundly. The far-away point, which is of no significance to us simply as far away, becomes of huge importance the moment we take it as defining a present direction of movement. Taken in this way it is no remote and distant result to be achieved, but a guiding method in dealing with the present. The systematized and defined experience of the adult mind, in other words, is of value to us in interpreting the child's life as it immediately shows itself, and in passing on to guidance or direction.

Let us look for a moment at these two ideas: interpretation and guidance. The child's present experience is in no way self-explanatory. It is not final, but transitional. It is nothing complete in itself, but just a sign or index of certain growth-tendencies. As long as we confine our gaze to what the child here and now puts forth, we are confused and misled. We cannot read its meaning. Extreme depreciations of the child morally and intellectually, and sentimental idealizations of him, have their root in a common fallacy. Both spring from taking stages of a growth or movement as something cut off and fixed. The first fails to see the promise contained in feelings and deeds which, taken by themselves, are uncompromising and repellent; the second fails to see that even the most pleasing and beautiful exhibitions are but

191

signs, and that they begin to spoil and rot the moment they are treated as achievements.

What we need is something which will enable us to interpret, to appraise, the elements in the child's present puttings forth and fallings away, his exhibitions of power and weakness, in the light of some larger growth-process in which they have their place. Only in this way can we discriminate. If we isolate the child's present inclinations, purposes, and experiences from the place they occupy and the part they have to perform in a developing experience, all stand upon the same level; all alike are equally good and equally bad. But in the movement of life different elements stand upon different planes of value. Some of the child's deeds are symptoms of a waning tendency; they are survivals in functioning of an organ which has done its part and is passing out of vital use. To give positive attention to such qualities is to arrest development upon a lower level. It is systematically to maintain a rudimentary phase of growth. Other activities are signs of a culminating power and interest; to them applies the maxim of striking while the iron is hot. As regards them, it is perhaps a matter of now or never. Selected, utilized, emphasized, they may mark a turning-point for good in the child's whole career; neglected, an opportunity goes, never to be recalled. Other acts and feelings are prophetic; they represent the dawning of flickering light that will shine steadily only in the far future. As regards them there is little at present to do but give them fair and full chance, waiting for the future for definite direction.

Just as, upon the whole, it was the weakness of the "old education" that it made invidious comparisons between the immaturity of the child and the maturity of the adult, regarding the former as something to be got away from as soon as possible and as much as possible; so it is the danger of the "new education" that it regard the child's present powers and interests as something finally significant in themselves. In truth, his learnings and achievements are fluid and moving. They change from day to day and from hour to hour.

It will do harm if child-study leave in the popular mind the impression that a child of a given age has a positive equipment of purposes and interests to be cultivated just as they stand. Interests in reality are but attitudes toward possible experiences; they are not achievements; their worth is in the leverage they afford, not in the accomplishment they represent. To take the phenomena presented at a given age as in any way self-explanatory or self-contained is inevitably to result in indulgence and spoiling. Any power, whether of child or adult, is indulged when it is taken on its given and present level in consciousness. Its genuine meaning is in the propulsion it affords toward a higher level. It is just something to do with. Appealing to the interest upon the present plane means excitation; it means playing with a power so as continually to stir it up without directing it toward definite achievement. Continuous initiation, continuous starting of activities that do not arrive, is, for all practical purposes, as bad as the continual repression of initiative in conformity with supposed interests of some more perfect thought or will. It is as if the child were forever tasting and never eating; always having his palate tickled upon the emotional side, but never getting the organic satisfaction that comes only with digestion of food and transformation of it into working power.

As against such a view, the subject-matter of science and history and art serves to reveal the real child to us. We do not know the meaning either of his tendencies or of his performances excepting as we take them as germinating seed, or opening bud, of some fruit to be borne. The whole world of visual nature is all too small an answer to the problem of the meaning of the child's instinct for light and form. The entire science of physics is none too much to interpret adequately to us what is involved in some simple demand of the child for explanation of some casual change that has attracted his attention. The art of Raphael or of Corot is none too much to enable us to value the impulses stirring in the child when he draws and daubs.

So much for the use of the subject-matter in interpretation. Its further employment in direction or guidance is but an expansion of the same thought. To interpret the fact is to see it in its vital movement, to see it in its relation to growth. But to view it as a part of a normal growth is to secure the basis for guiding it. Guidance is not external imposition. *It is freeing the life-process for its own most adequate fulfilment.* What was said about disregard of the child's present experience because of its remoteness from mature experience; and of the sentimental idealization of the child's naïve caprices and performances, may be repeated here with slightly altered phrase. There are those who see no alternative between forcing the child from without, or leaving him entirely alone. Seeing no alternative, some choose one mode, some another. Both fall into the same fundamental error. Both fail to see that development is a definite process, having its own law which can be fulfilled only when adequate and normal conditions are provided. Really to interpret the child's present crude impulses in counting, measuring, and arranging things in rhythmic series involves mathematical scholarship—a knowledge of the mathematical formulae and relations which have, in the history of the race, grown out of just such crude beginnings. To see the whole history of development which intervenes between these two terms is simply to see what step the child needs to take just here and now; to what use he needs to put his blind impulse in order that it may get clarity and gain force.

If, once more, the "old education" tended to ignore the dynamic quality, the developing force inherent in the child's present experience, and therefore to assume that direction and control were just matters of arbitrarily putting the child in a given path and compelling him to walk there, the "new education" is in danger of taking the idea of development in altogether too formal and empty a way. The child is expected to "develop" this or that fact or truth out of his own mind. He is told to think things out, or work things out for himself, without being supplied any of the environing conditions which are requisite to start and guide thought. Nothing can be developed from nothing; nothing but the crude can be developed out of the crude—and this is what surely happens when we throw the child back upon his achieved self as a finality, and invite him to spin new truths of nature or of conduct out of that. It is certainly as futile to expect a child to evolve a universe out of his own mere mind as it is for a philosopher to attempt that task. Development does not mean just getting something out of the mind. It is a development of experience and into experience that is really wanted. And this is impossible save as just that educative medium is provided which will enable the powers and interests that have been selected as valuable to function. They must operate, and how they operate will depend almost entirely upon the stimuli which surround them and the material upon which they exercise themselves. The problem of direction is thus the problem of selecting appropriate stimuli for instincts and impulses which it is desired to employ in the gaining of new experience. What new experiences are desirable, and thus what stimuli are needed, it is impossible to tell except as there is some comprehension of the development which is aimed at; except, in a word, as the adult knowledge is drawn upon as revealing the possible career open to the child.

It may be of use to distinguish and to relate to each other the logical and the psychological aspects of experience—the former standing for subject-matter in itself, the latter for it in relation to the child. A psychological statement of experience follows its actual growth; it is historic; it notes steps actually taken, the uncertain and tortuous, as well as the efficient and successful. The logical point of view, on the other hand, assumes that the development has reached a certain positive stage of fulfilment. It neglects the process and considers the outcome. It summarizes and arranges, and thus separates the achieved results from the actual steps by which they were forthcoming in the first instance. We may compare the difference between the logical and the psychological to the difference between the notes which an explorer makes in a new country, blazing a trail and finding his way along as best he may, and the finished map that is constructed after the country has been thoroughly explored. The two are mutually dependent. Without the more or less accidental and devious paths traced by the explorer there would be no facts which could be utilized in the making of the complete and related chart. But no

197

one would get the benefit of the explorer's trip if it was not compared and checked up with similar wanderings undertaken by others; unless the new geographical facts learned, the streams crossed, the mountains climbed, etc., were viewed, not as mere incidents in the journey of the particular traveler, but (quite apart from the individual explorer's life) in relation to other similar facts already known. The map orders individual experiences, connecting them with one another irrespective of the local and temporal circumstances and accidents of their original discovery.

Of what use is this formulated statement of experience? Of what use is the map?

Well, we may first tell what the map is not. The map is not a substitute for a personal experience. The map does not take the place of an actual journey. The logically formulated material of a science or branch of learning, of a study, is no substitute for the having of individual experiences. The mathematical formula for a falling body does not take the place of personal contact and immediate individual experience with the falling thing. But the map, a summary, an arranged and orderly view of previous experiences, serves as a guide to future experience; it gives direction; it facilitates control; it economizes effort, preventing useless wandering, and pointing out the paths which lead most quickly and most certainly to a desired result. Through the map every new traveler may get for his own journey the benefits of the results of others' explorations without the waste of energy and loss of time involved in their wanderings—wanderings which he himself would be obliged to repeat were it not for just the assistance of the objective and generalized record of their performances. That which we call a science or study puts the net product of past experience in the form which makes it most available for the future. It represents a capitalization which may at once be turned to interest. It economizes the workings of the mind in every way. Memory is less taxed because the facts are grouped together about some common principle, instead of being connected solely with the varying incidents of their original discovery. Observation is assisted; we know what to look for and where to look. It is the difference between looking for a needle in a haystack, and searching for a given paper in a well-arranged cabinet. Reasoning is directed, because there is a certain general path or line laid out along which ideas naturally march, instead of moving from one chance association to another.

There is, then, nothing final about a logical rendering of experience. Its value is not contained in itself; its significance is that of standpoint, outlook, method. It intervenes between the more casual, tentative, and roundabout experiences of the past, and more controlled and orderly experiences of the future. It gives past experience in that net form which renders it most available and most significant, most fecund for future experience. The abstractions, generalizations, and classifications which it introduces all have prospective meaning.

The formulated result is then not to be opposed to the process of growth. The logical is not set over against the psychological. The surveyed and arranged result occupies a critical position in the process of growth. It marks a turning-point. It shows how we may get the benefit of past effort in controlling future endeavor. In the largest sense the logical standpoint is itself psychological; it has its meaning as a point in the development of experience, and its justification is in its functioning in the future growth which it insures.

Hence the need of reinstating into experience the subject-matter of the studies, or branches of learning. It must be restored to the experience from which it has been abstracted. It needs to be *psychologized*; turned over, translated into the immediate and individual experiencing within which it has its origin and significance.

Every study or subject thus has two aspects: one for the scientist as a scientist; the other for the teacher as a teacher. These two aspects are in no sense opposed or conflicting. But neither are they immediately identical. For the scientist, the subject-matter represents simply a given body of truth to be employed in locating new problems, instituting new researches, and carrying them through to a verified outcome. To him the subject-matter of the science is self-contained. He refers various portions of it to each other; he connects new facts with it. He is not, as a scientist, called upon to travel outside its particular bounds; if he does, it is only to get more facts of the same general sort. The problem of the teacher is a different one. As a teacher he is not concerned with adding new facts to the science he teaches; in propounding new hypotheses or in verifying them. He is concerned with the subject-matter of the science as *representing a given stage and phase of the development of experience*. His problem is that of inducing a vital and personal experiencing. Hence, what concerns him, as teacher, is the ways in which that subject may become a part of experience; what there is in the child's present that is usable with reference to it; how such elements are to be used; how his own knowledge of the subject-matter may assist in interpreting the child's needs and doings, and determine the medium in which the child should be placed in order that his growth may be properly directed. He is concerned, not with the subject-matter as such, but with the subject-matter as a related factor in a total and growing experience. Thus to see it is to psychologize it.

It is the failure to keep in mind the double aspect of subject-matter which causes the curriculum and child to be set over against each other as described in our early pages. The subject-matter, just as it is for the scientist, has no direct relationship to the child's present experience. It stands outside of it. The danger here is not a merely theoretical one. We are practically threatened on all sides. Textbook and teacher vie with each other in presenting to the child the subject-matter as it stands to the specialist. Such modification and revision as it undergoes are a mere elimination of certain scientific difficulties, and the general reduction to a lower intellectual level. The material is not translated into life-terms, but is directly offered as a substitute for, or an external annex to, the child's present life.

Three typical evils result: In the first place, the lack of any organic connection with what the child has already seen and felt and loved makes the material purely formal and symbolic. There is a sense in which it is impossible to value too highly the formal and the symbolic. The genuine form, the real symbol, serve as methods in the holding and discovery of truth. They are tools by which the individual pushes out most surely and widely into unexplored areas. They are means by which he brings to bear whatever of reality he has succeeded in gaining in past searchings. But this happens only when the symbol really symbolizes—when it stands for and sums up in shorthand actual experiences which the individual has already gone through. A symbol which is induced from without, which has not been led up to in preliminary activities, is, as we say, a bare or mere symbol; it is dead and barren. Now, any fact, whether of arithmetic, or geography, or grammar, which is not led up to and into out of something which has previously occupied a significant position in the child's life for its own sake, is forced into this position. It is not a reality, but just the sign of a reality which *might* be experienced if certain conditions were fulfilled. But the abrupt presentation of the fact as something known by others, and requiring only to be studied and learned by the child, rules out such conditions of fulfilment. It condemns the fact to be a hieroglyph: it would mean something if one only had the key. The clue being lacking, it remains an idle curiosity, to fret and obstruct the mind, a dead weight to burden it.

The second evil in this external presentation is lack of motivation. There are not only no facts or truths which have been previously felt as such with which to appropriate and assimilate the new, but there is no craving, no need, no demand. When the subject-matter has been psychologized, that is, viewed as an outgrowth of present tendencies and activities, it is easy to locate in the present some obstacle, intellectual, practical, or ethical, which can be handled more adequately if the truth in question be mastered. This need supplies motive for the learning. An end which is the child's own carries him on to possess the means of its accomplishment. But when material is directly supplied in the form of a lesson to be learned as a lesson, the connecting links of need and aim are conspicuous for their absence. What we mean by the mechanical and dead in instruction is a result of this lack of motivation. The organic and vital mean interaction—they mean play of mental demand and material supply.

The third evil is that even the most scientific matter, arranged in most logical fashion, loses this quality, when presented in external, ready-made fashion, by the time it gets to the child. It has to undergo some modification in order to shut out some phases too hard to grasp, and to reduce some of the attendant difficulties. What happens? Those things which are most significant to the scientific man, and most valuable in the logic of actual inquiry and classification, drop out. The really thought-provoking character is obscured, and the organizing function disappears. Or, as we commonly say, the child's reasoning powers, the faculty of abstraction and generalization, are not adequately developed. So the subject-matter is evacuated of its logical value, and, though it is what it is only from the logical standpoint, is presented as stuff only for "memory." This is the contradiction: the child gets the advantage neither of the adult logical formulation, nor of his own native competencies of apprehension and response. Hence the logic of the child is hampered and mortified, and we are almost fortunate if he does not get actual non-science, flat and commonplace residua of what was gaining scientific vitality a generation or two ago—degenerate reminiscence of what someone else once formulated on the basis of the experience that some further person had, once upon a time, experienced.

The train of evils does not cease. It is all too common for opposed erroneous theories to play straight into each other's hands. Psychological considerations may be slurred or shoved one side; they cannot be crowded out. Put out of the door, they come back through the window. Somehow and somewhere motive must be appealed to, connection must be established between the mind and its material. There is no question of getting along without this bond of connection; the only question is whether it be such as grows out of the material itself in relation to the mind, or be imported and hitched on from some outside source. If the subject-matter of the lessons be such as to have an appropriate place within the expanding consciousness of the child, if it grows out of his own past doings, thinkings, and sufferings, and grows into application in further achievements and receptivities, then no device or trick of method has to be resorted to in order to enlist "interest." The psychologized *is* of interest—that is, it is placed in the whole of conscious life so that it shares the worth of that life. But the externally presented material, conceived and generated in standpoints and attitudes remote from the child, and developed in motives alien to him, has no such place of its own. Hence the recourse to adventitious leverage to push it in, to factitious drill to drive it in, to artificial bribe to lure it in.

Three aspects of this recourse to outside ways for giving the subject-matter some psychological meaning may be worth mentioning. Familiarity breeds contempt, but it also breeds something like affection. We get used to the chains we wear, and we miss them when removed. 'Tis an old story that through custom we finally embrace what at first wore a hideous mien. Unpleasant, because meaningless, activities may get agreeable if long enough persisted in. *It is possible for the mind to develop interest in a routine or mechanical procedure if conditions are continually supplied which demand that mode of operation and preclude any other sort.* I frequently hear dulling devices and empty exercises defended and extolled because "the children take such an 'interest' in them." Yes, that is the worst of it; the mind, shut out from worthy employ and missing the taste of adequate performance, comes down to the level of that which is left to it to know and do, and perforce takes an interest in a cabined and cramped experience. To find satisfaction in its own exercise is the normal law of mind, and if large and meaningful business for the mind be denied, it tries to content itself with the formal movements that remain to it—and too often succeeds, save in those cases of more intense activity which cannot accommodate themselves, and that make up the unruly and *declassé* of our school product. An interest in the formal apprehension of symbols and in their memorized reproduction becomes in many pupils a substitute for the original and vital interest in reality; and all because, the subject-matter of the course of study being out of relation to the concrete mind of the individual, some substitute bond to hold it in some kind of working relation to the mind must be discovered and elaborated.

The second substitute for living motivation in the subject-matter is that of contrast-effects; the material of the lesson is rendered interesting, if not in itself, at least in contrast with some alternative experience. To learn the lesson is more interesting than to take a scolding, be held up to general ridicule, stay after school, receive degradingly low marks, or fail to be promoted. And very much of what goes by the name of "discipline," and prides itself upon opposing the doctrines of a soft pedagogy and upon upholding the banner of effort and duty, is nothing more or less than just this appeal to "interest" in its obverse aspect— to fear, to dislike of various kinds of physical, social, and personal pain. The subject-matter does not appeal; it cannot appeal; it lacks origin and bearing in a growing experience. So the appeal is to the thousand and one outside and irrelevant agencies which may serve to throw, by sheer rebuff and rebound, the mind back upon the material from which it is constantly wandering.

Human nature being what it is, however, it tends to seek its motivation in the agreeable rather than in the disagreeable, in direct pleasure rather than in alternative pain. And so has come up the modern theory and practice of the "interesting," in the false sense of that term. The material is still left; so far as its own characteristics are concerned, just material externally selected and formulated. It is still just so much geography and arithmetic and grammar study; not so much potentiality of child-experience with regard to language, earth, and numbered and measured reality. Hence the difficulty of bringing the mind to bear upon it; hence its repulsiveness; the tendency for attention to wander; for other acts and images to crowd in and expel the lesson. The legitimate way out is to transform the material; to psychologize it—that is, once more, to take it and to develop it within the range and scope of the child's life. But it is easier and simpler to leave it as it is, and then by trick of method to arouse interest, to make it *interesting*; to cover it with sugar-coating; to conceal its barrenness by intermediate and unrelated material; and finally, as it were, to get the child to swallow and digest the unpalatable morsel while he is enjoying tasting something quite different. But alas for the analogy! Mental assimilation is a matter of consciousness; and if the attention has not been playing upon the actual material, that has not been apprehended, nor worked into faculty.

How, then, stands the case of Child *vs.* Curriculum? What shall the verdict be? The radical fallacy in the original pleadings with which we set out is the supposition that we have no choice save either to leave the child to his own unguided spontaneity or to inspire direction upon him from without. Action is response; it is adaptation, adjustment. There is no such thing as sheer self-activity possible—because all activity takes place in a medium, in a situation, and with reference to its conditions. But, again, no such thing as imposition of truth from without, as insertion of truth from without, is possible. All depends upon the activity which the mind itself undergoes in responding to what is presented from without. Now, the value of the formulated wealth of knowledge that makes up the course of study is that it may enable the educator *to determine the environment of the child,* and thus by indirection to direct. Its primary value, its primary indication, is for the teacher, not for the child. It says to the teacher: Such and such are the capacities, the fulfilments, in truth and beauty and behavior, open to these children. Now see to it that day by day the conditions are such that *their own activities* move inevitably in this direction, toward such culmination of themselves. Let the child's nature fulfil its own destiny, revealed to you in whatever of science and art and industry the world now holds as its own.

The case is of Child. It is his present powers which are to assert themselves; his present capacities which are to be exercised; his present attitudes which are to be realized. But save as the teacher knows, knows wisely and thoroughly, the race-expression which is embodied in that thing we call the Curriculum, the teacher knows neither what the present power, capacity, or attitude is, nor yet how it is to be asserted, exercised, and realized.